TECHNICAL REPORT

# Building Community Resilience to Disasters

## A Way Forward to Enhance National Health Security

*Anita Chandra • Joie Acosta • Stefanie Stern • Lori Uscher-Pines*
*Malcolm V. Williams • Douglas Yeung • Jeffrey Garnett • Lisa S. Meredith*

Sponsored by the U.S. Department of Health and Human Services

RAND HEALTH

This work was sponsored by the U.S. Department of Health and Human Services. The research was conducted in RAND Health, a division of the RAND Corporation.

**Library of Congress Cataloging-in-Publication Data** is available for this publication.

ISBN 978-0-8330-5195-0

The RAND Corporation is a nonprofit institution that helps improve policy and decisionmaking through research and analysis. RAND's publications do not necessarily reflect the opinions of its research clients and sponsors.

**RAND®** is a registered trademark.

*Cover: Survivors of Hurricane Katrina arrive at New Orleans Airport where FEMA's D-MAT teams have set up a medical hospital and where people will be flown to shelters in other states, September 1, 2005. FEMA photo by Michael Rieger.*

Published 2011 by the RAND Corporation
1776 Main Street, P.O. Box 2138, Santa Monica, CA 90407-2138
1200 South Hayes Street, Arlington, VA 22202-5050
4570 Fifth Avenue, Suite 600, Pittsburgh, PA 15213-2665
RAND URL: http://www.rand.org/
To order RAND documents or to obtain additional information, contact
Distribution Services: Telephone: (310) 451-7002;
Fax: (310) 451-6915; Email: order@rand.org

# Preface

Community resilience, or the sustained ability of a community to withstand and recover from adversity (e.g., economic stress, influenza pandemic, man-made or natural disasters) has become a key policy issue, which is being embraced at federal, state, and local levels. Given that resources are limited in the wake of an emergency, it is increasingly recognized that resilience is considered critical to a community's ability to reduce long recovery periods after an emergency. The goal of this report is to provide a roadmap for federal, state, and local leaders who are developing plans to enhance community resilience for health security threats. The report describes options for building community resilience in key areas. We provide a definition of community resilience in the context of national health security and a set of eight levers and five core components for building resilience. We describe suggested activities that communities are pursuing and may want to strengthen for community resilience, and we identify challenges to implementation.

This research was conducted from October 2009 through October 2010. It was sponsored by the U.S. Department of Health and Human Services Assistant Secretary for Preparedness and Response and was carried out within the RAND Health Public Health Systems and Preparedness Initiative. RAND Health is a division of the RAND Corporation. A profile of the Center, abstracts of its publications, and ordering information can be found at http://www.rand.org/health/centers/preparedness/. More information about RAND is available at www.rand.org. Comments or inquiries should be sent to the report's lead author, Anita Chandra (Anita_Chandra@rand.org), or the principal investigator of the larger project of which this report is but one part: Jeffery Wasserman (Jeffrey_Wasserman@rand.org). The mailing address is RAND Corporation, 1776 Main Street, P.O. Box 2138, Santa Monica, CA 90407. More information about RAND is available at http://www.rand.org.

# Contents

# Figures

# Tables

# Summary

Community resilience, or the sustained ability of a community to withstand and recover from adversity (e.g., economic stress, influenza pandemic, man-made or natural disasters), has become a key policy issue, especially in recent years (HHS, 2009; National Security Strategy, 2010; DHS, 2010a). This emphasis on resilience is being embraced at federal (Department of Health and Human Services [HHS], Department of Homeland Security [DHS], the White House), state, and local levels. The National Health Security Strategy (NHSS) (HHS, 2009) identifies community resilience as critical to national health security, i.e., ensuring that the nation is prepared for, protected from, and able to respond to and recover from incidents with potentially negative health consequences. Given that resources are limited in the wake of an emergency, it is increasingly recognized that communities may need to be on their own after an emergency before help arrives, and thus need to build resilience before an emergency. Resilience is also considered critical to a community's ability to reduce long recovery periods after an emergency, which can otherwise require a significant amount of time and resources at the federal, state, and local levels.

While there is general consensus that *community resilience* is defined as the ability of communities to withstand and mitigate the stress of a disaster, there is less clarity on the precise resilience-building process. In other words, we have limited understanding about the components that can be changed or the "levers" for action that enable communities to recover more quickly. The literature to date has identified factors likely to be correlated with achieving resilience for communities, including reducing pre-disaster vulnerabilities and conducting pre-event prevention activities to minimize the negative consequences of disaster; however, these domains have been rather broad and lack the specificity required for implementation. Further, community resilience in the context of health security represents a unique intersection of preparedness/emergency management, traditional public health, and community development, with its emphasis on preventive care, health promotion, and community capacity-building. Thus, addressing the national goal of building community resilience (as outlined in the NHSS) offers an opportunity for communities to identify and build on the public health activities that local health departments and their partners are already pursuing. Community resilience is a relatively new term for the public health community, but it captures and expands upon many traditional themes in emergency preparedness as well as general health promotion. In the context of today's resource-limited environment where efficiency is critical, communities can identify and leverage the activities that are already in place to further build resilience.

Although the importance of community resilience to health security is widely recognized, understanding how to leverage existing programs and resources to build community resilience is a significant challenge. Important community tools have been developed to assist communities in enhancing aspects of resilience, and they should be used. They include the Community

Advancing Resilience Toolkit (CART) and the work by the Community and Regional Resilience Institute (CARRI).

However, a roadmap or initial list of activities that communities could implement to bolster community resilience *specific* to national health security is still needed. Several important assumptions motivate the need for this roadmap. Despite progress in identifying the conceptual and theoretical underpinnings of community resilience, a working definition of community resilience in the context of health security has been lacking. Further, we acknowledge that communities have been implementing many strategies to enhance their resilience. However, it is difficult for local health departments and their partners to synthesize the wealth of information from the current body of literature and place it within the context of national health security in a way that will inform local planning. To date, communities have minimal opportunity to share activities for building or enhancing community resilience and to discuss whether and how government and nongovernmental actors should be involved. Further, it is currently unclear how to measure community resilience to assess the level of progress toward achieving greater health security.

This report provides an initial model of options for building community resilience in key areas. Note that in certain circumstances, communities have already undertaken activities similar to those listed herein. This report is intended to be comprehensive, and therefore it provides a menu of options that can be prioritized.

The report is intended principally for community leaders developing a local strategy for building resilience. These leaders include government and nongovernment actors who may be part of local emergency planning committees or related community planning teams. Given the limited evidence base on what activities are most effective for bolstering community resilience, the report is not intended as an implementation guide or "how to" toolkit. Although the goal of the report is to provide information to motivate local planning, it will be incumbent upon communities to critically review the information, assess the activities they are already undertaking, select from newly identified activities with attention to which activities are feasible given resource constraints, develop locally driven plans, test activities, and share lessons learned with other communities.

For this study, we performed three tasks: (1) conducted a substantive literature review, (2) convened six stakeholder focus groups across the United States, and (3) held three meetings with relevant subject matter experts (SMEs). The definition of community resilience and the activities we outline here for achieving resilience were created in consultation with outside experts representing various stakeholder groups in public health, medicine, social services, and emergency management.

## Definition of Community Resilience in the Context of National Health Security

The definition of community resilience is shown in the box. The definition draws upon both the literature review (Norris, 2008; Chandra et al., 2010; HHS, 2009; HHS, 2010a), as well as discussions with focus group participants.

---

**Definition of Community Resilience**

**Main Definition:**

*Community resilience entails the ongoing and developing capacity of the community to account for its vulnerabilities and develop capabilities that aid that community in (1) preventing, withstanding, and mitigating the stress of a health incident; (2) recovering in a way that restores the community to a state of self-sufficiency and at least the same level of health and social functioning after a health incident; and (3) using knowledge from a past response to strengthen the community's ability to withstand the next health incident.*

**Key Components:**

Key components or "building blocks" of community resilience that affect both a community's pre-event vulnerability to disaster and its adaptive capacity to recover include the physical and psychological health of the population; social and economic well-being; individual, family, and community knowledge and attitudes regarding self-reliance and self-help; effective risk communication; level of social integration of government and nongovernmental organizations in planning, response, and recovery; and the social connectedness of community members. In order to build community resilience, a community must develop capabilities in the following areas: active engagement of community stakeholders in health event planning and personal preparedness, development of social networks, creation of health-promoting opportunities to improve the physical and psychological health of the community (as well as to address disparities in health across subgroups), plans and programs that address and support the functional needs of at-risk individuals (including children), institution of plans to respond effectively to the post-disaster physical and psychological health needs of community members, and rebuilding plans for health and social systems that can be activated immediately.

---

The definition emphasizes the following concepts, which focus group participants suggested would be evident in a resilient community:

- Engagement at the community level, including a sense of cohesiveness and neighborhood involvement or integration
- Partnership among organizations, including integrated pre-event planning, exercises, and agreements
- Sustained local leadership supported by partnership with state and federal government
- Effective and culturally relevant education about risks
- Optimal community health and access to quality health services
- Integration of preparedness and wellness
- Rapid restoration of services and social networks
- Individual-level preparedness and self-sufficiency
- Targeted strategies that empower and engage vulnerable populations
- Financial resiliency of families and businesses, and efficient leveraging of resources for recovery.

We acknowledge that the definition of "community" can widely vary; it can be a geographic term or can be bounded by membership to a cultural group. Although it will be important for local planning teams to define community boundaries with community stakeholders, for the purpose of this roadmap, we primarily use a geographic definition guided by the catchment area of the local health department (e.g., city/county/parish/municipality).

## Levers for Building Community Resilience

To identify key activities for building and strengthening community resilience, we drew on findings from the literature review, focus groups, and SME meetings to define eight "levers" that can be used by communities to strengthen community resilience in the context of the health security. These levers are shown in the rounded boxes in Figure S.1.

The levers are designed to strengthen the five core components (shown in rectangular boxes), which are correlated with community resilience in the specific context of enhancing health security or public health preparedness. The *components* are the main domains or factors associated with community resilience, such as the health of the population. The *levers* are the means of reaching the components, such as improving a population's access to health services. The levers are highlighted in boldface type below:

- **Wellness** and **access** contribute to the development of the social and economic well-being of a community and the physical and psychological health of the population.
- Specific to the disaster experience, **education** can be used to improve effective risk communication, **engagement** and **self-sufficiency** are needed to build social connectedness, and **partnership** helps ensure that government and nongovernmental organizations (NGOs) are integrated and involved in resilience-building and disaster planning.

**Figure S.1**
**Levers and Core Components of Community Resilience**

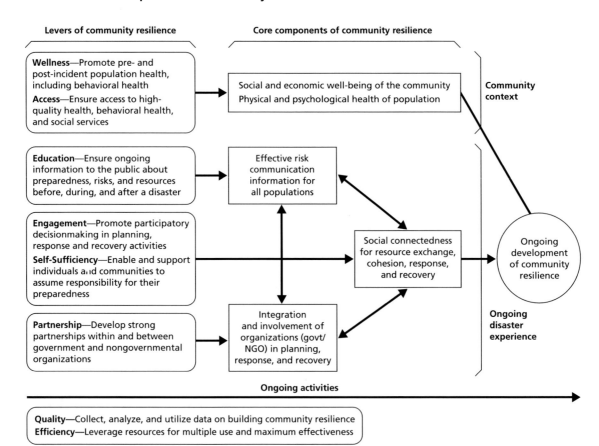

- **Quality** and **efficiency** are ongoing levers that cut across all levers and core components of community resilience.

### Activities for Building Community Resilience

Because activities related to the levers strengthen each of the components of community resilience, a community moves closer to achieving community resilience as it conducts more activities. This process is shown in a circle in Figure S.1 because developing resilience is not static but rather is an iterative and ongoing process.

The main body of this report (Chapters Three through Ten) describes suggested activities that communities can use or build on to strengthen community resilience in specific areas. The activities presented in the report offer a range of ideas that can be implemented by communities according to their specific needs. It will be important for communities to use the roadmap as a starting point for local community resilience strategy development (see next section). None of these activities has undergone rigorous evaluation. Before a community resilience *toolkit* can be developed, communities will need to use this roadmap, report on lessons learned, and assess the impact of implementing particular activities (see Appendix C for a community prioritization tool).

## Implementation and Measurement of Community Resilience–Building Activities

As communities review this roadmap, it is important to determine an approach to implementation, including monitoring and evaluating implementation and determining the effectiveness of particular activities. These implementation questions include the following:

- How will we know if these activities are working?
- What capacities are needed for communities to fully implement community resilience–building activities?
- How long will it take communities to achieve full implementation of community resilience–building activities?

### How Will We Know If Community Resilience–Building Activities Are Working?

Measurement of community resilience is essential for the operationalization and implementation of community resilience. Measurement will allow communities, states, and the nation as a whole to assess hypothesized links between inputs into the community resilience process (e.g., community partnerships and education of community members) and outcomes (e.g., greater resilience). Measurement is also critical to track progress in building community resilience at the local level. In Chapter Eleven, we suggest some potential areas of measurement for community resilience. Testing of proposed measures will be needed to develop the evidence base, refine the measures, and inform the next generation of measures.

### What Capacities Are Needed for Communities to Fully Implement Community Resilience–Building Activities?

Much as in traditional public health practice, implementing community resilience–building activities requires the capacity to build and maintain strong and reliable partnerships (e.g., the partnership lever), mobilize community members (e.g., the engagement lever), and use data and information for evaluation, monitoring, and decisionmaking (e.g., the quality lever). Strong and reliable partnerships involve a diverse array of public, private, governmental, and nongovernmental organizations (e.g., academic institutions, healthcare providers, advocacy groups, media outlets, businesses). In building partnerships, communities will have to consider such questions as who should take the lead in establishing partnerships and how community resilience–building activities might need to be adapted for specific communities. Engagement and self-sufficiency also require the capacity to mobilize partnerships. Models such as the Mobilizing for Action through Planning and Partnership (MAPP) have been developed to support community mobilization efforts (Mays, 2010). Finally, state and local health agencies are increasingly utilizing performance standards, measures, monitoring, and quality improvement processes.

### How Long Will It Take for Communities to Achieve Full Implementation of Community Resilience–Building Activities?

Implementing community resilience activities takes time. In order to appropriately gauge expectations, a richer understanding of the process of implementation is needed. In addition, implementation planning should acknowledge the activities that communities are already pursuing to enhance resilience. It can be helpful to draw guidance from a model of implementation that outlines the stages that a community must pass through before *full implementation* is achieved (Simpson, 2002). One such model is the Simpson Transfer Model, in which diffusion happens in four stages: exposure, adoption, implementation, and practice (Simpson, 2002). Communities must first be exposed to community resilience–building and then can build the capacity needed to adopt activities to build resilience. Once organizations have the capacity to implement community resilience–building activities, they begin early implementation, followed by practice of the activities until they become institutionalized. Appropriate monitoring and evaluation can help communities assess what stage of implementation they are in and gauge outcomes accordingly.

## Conclusion and Future Research Directions

This roadmap represents an important step forward in identifying the critical elements of community resilience to support national health security and offers a practical list of potential activities for building resilience before a disaster. The report also suggests several areas in which the evidence base for community resilience needs to be strengthened. Clarification in such areas as the following should identify best practices in community resilience-building and measure the overall effect of increasing community resilience:

**Wellness and Access:** What are the best ways to frame preparedness in the context of wellness messaging? How should communities convey the connection between individual/family and community preparedness?

**Education:** How do we link better risk communication with improved community resilience?

**Engagement:** How can we use advanced technologies, including new social media, to inform the public, facilitate the social re-engagement of people after a disaster, and promote social connectedness?

**Self-Sufficiency:** What are the best means to incentivize individual and community preparedness? What policies, including financial and other incentives, will work?

**Partnership:** What is the best way to integrate nongovernmental organizations in planning, and what is the most effective way to assess the capacities and capabilities of specific NGO partners?

**Quality and Efficiency:** What are the best metrics for monitoring and evaluating resilience–building activities? Which baseline data are most critical for assessing key community resilience components and elements?

# Acknowledgments

We extend our sincere appreciation to the U.S. Department of Health and Human Servicess Assistant Secretary for Preparedness and Response for supporting this research. In particular, we thank Jonathan Ban, Daniel Dodgen, Darrin Donato, and Rachel Kaul for their collaboration. We also thank Lois Davis, Oksana Hucul, and Fran Norris for their critical review of this report. In addition, we thank Kristin Leuschner for her input on the design and content of the report. Most importantly, we thank state and local leaders who provided input via focus groups and subject matter expert meetings.

# Abbreviations

| | |
|---|---|
| BRFSS | Behavioral Risk Factor Surveillance System |
| CARRI | Community and Regional Resilience Institute |
| CQI | continuous quality improvement |
| DHS | Department of Homeland Security |
| FEMA | Federal Emergency Management Agency |
| HHS | Department of Health and Human Services |
| LEPC | Local Emergency Planning Committee |
| MAPP | Mobilizing for Action through Planning and Partnership |
| NEMIS | National Emergency Management Information System |
| NHSS | National Health Security Strategy |
| NGO | nongovernmental organization |
| OPEO | Office of Preparedness and Emergency Operations |

# CHAPTER ONE

# Introduction

Community resilience, or the sustained ability of a community to withstand and recover from adversity (e.g., economic stress, influenza pandemic, man-made or natural disasters) has become a key policy issue, especially in recent years (HHS, 2009; National Security Strategy, 2010; DHS, 2010a). This emphasis on resilience is being embraced at federal (Department of Health and Human Servicesf [HHS], Department of Homeland Security [DHS], the White House), state, and local levels. The National Health Security Strategy (NHSS) identifies community resilience as critical to national health security, i.e., ensuring that the nation is prepared for, protected from, and able to respond to and recover from incidents with potentially negative health consequences. Given that resources are limited in the wake of an emergency, it is increasingly recognized that communities may need to be on their own after an emergency before help arrives and thus need to build resilience before an emergency. Resilience is also considered critical to a community's ability to reduce long recovery periods after an emergency, which can otherwise require a significant amount of time and resources at the federal, state, and local levels.

While there is general consensus that *community resilience* is defined as the ability of communities to withstand and mitigate the stress of a disaster, there is less clarity on the precise resilience-building process. In other words, we have limited understanding about the components that can be changed or the "levers" for action that enable communities to recover more quickly. The literature to date has identified factors likely to be correlated with achieving resilience for communities, including reducing pre-disaster vulnerabilities and conducting pre-event prevention activities to minimize the negative consequences of disaster; however, domains have been rather broad and lacking the specificity required for implementation. Further, community resilience in the context of health security represents a unique intersection of preparedness/emergency management, traditional public health, and community development, with its emphasis on preventive care, health promotion, and community capacity-building. Thus, addressing the national goal of building community resilience (as outlined in the NHSS) offers an opportunity for communities to identify and build on the public health activities that local health departments and their partners are already pursuing. "Community resilience" is a relatively new term for the public health community, but it captures and expands upon many traditional themes in emergency preparedness as well as general health promotion. In the context of today's resource-limited environment where efficiency is critical, communities can identify and leverage the activities that are already in place to further build resilience.

Although the importance of community resilience to health security is widely recognized, understanding how to leverage existing programs and resources to build community resilience is a significant challenge. Important community tools have been developed to assist communities in enhancing aspects of resilience, and they should be used. They include the Community Advancing Resilience Toolkit (CART) and the work by the Community and Regional Resilience Institute (CARRI).

However, a roadmap or initial list of activities that communities could implement to bolster community resilience *specific* to national health security is still needed. Several important assumptions motivate the need for this roadmap. Despite progress in identifying the conceptual and theoretical underpinnings of community resilience, a working definition of community resilience in the context of health security has been lacking. Further, we acknowledge that communities have already been implementing many strategies to enhance their resilience. However, it is difficult for local health departments and their partners to synthesize the wealth of information from the current body of literature and place it within the context of national health security in a way that will inform local planning. To date, communities have minimal opportunity to share activities to build or enhance community resilience and to discuss whether and how government and nongovernmental actors should be involved. Further, it is currently unclear how to measure community resilience to assess the level of progress toward achieving greater health security.

## Focus of This Report

This report provides an initial model of options for building community resilience in key areas. Note that in certain circumstances, communities will already have undertaken activities similar to those listed in this report. This report is meant to be comprehensive and therefore provides a menu of options that can be prioritized.

The report is intended principally for community leaders developing a local strategy for building resilience. These leaders include government and nongovernment actors who may be part of local emergency planning committees or related community-planning teams. Given the limited evidence base on what activities are most effective for bolstering community resilience, the report is not intended as an implementation guide or "how to" toolkit. Although its goal is to provide information to motivate local planning, it will be incumbent upon communities to critically review the information, assess the activities they are already undertaking, select from new identified activities with attention to which activities are feasible given resource constraints, develop locally driven plans, test activities, and share lessons learned with other communities (see "Using This Report Checklist" at the end of Chapter One). The report addresses three main issues.

First, we provide a definition of community resilience in the context of national health security and a set of five core components and eight levers for building resilience (see Figure 1.1 for definitions of terms). The components are the main domains or factors associated with community resilience, such as the health of the population. The levers are the means of reaching the components, such as improving a population's access to health services (Chapter Two).

Next, we describe suggested activities that communities can take to build and strengthen community resilience, organized in relation to the eight levers of resilience. These chapters (Three through Ten) are divided by lever and stem from the literature review and community stakeholder meetings described in the next section. Within each chapter, we describe the ele-

**Figure 1.1
Definitions of Community Resilience Terms Used in This Report**

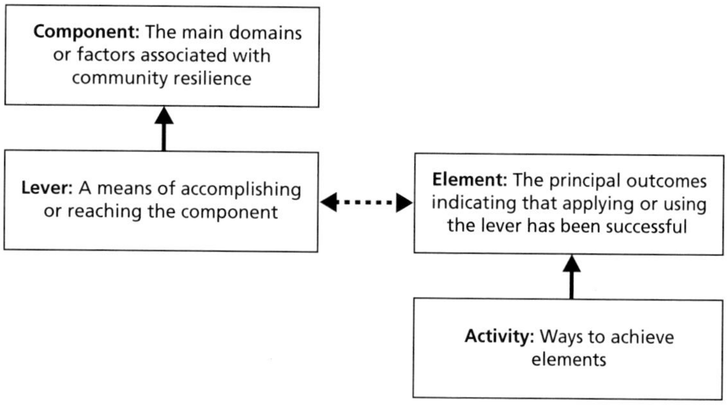

ments (the principal outcomes indicating that applying or using the lever has been successful) and list activities (ways to achieve elements) that could be used by communities.

These stakeholder meetings included state and local leaders and subject matter experts (SMEs). Our objective in this section of the report (Chapters Three through Ten) is to provide results from our canvas or review of community resilience-building activities currently underway or considered important for health security by community stakeholders. Communities will vary in how they select the levers to target and which activities will strengthen that lever based on their community risk profile and needs. Activities can be implemented by both governmental and nongovernmental organizations (the latter including both nonprofits as well as private businesses). Some activities are directed toward state or federal government.

Finally, in Chapter Eleven we identify some challenges to implementing community resilience activities and propose some research directions that might be pursued in the future, including testing community resilience activities and further understanding how different components of resilience fit together. This final chapter will be of interest to public health researchers, federal stakeholders, and funders as well as community leaders.

## Approach

For this study, we performed three tasks: (1) conducted a substantive literature review, (2) convened six stakeholder focus groups from across the United States, and (3) held three meetings with relevant SMEs. The definition of community resilience and the activities we outline here for achieving resilience were created in consultation with outside experts representing various stakeholder groups in public health, medicine, social services, and emergency management.

### Literature Review

We examined peer-reviewed and published but not peer-reviewed ("gray") literature (available from January 1, 1996, through December 31, 2009) to identify factors associated with community resilience and to inform recommendations for measuring community resilience. In the literature review, we focused on factors most closely related to health security, public health, or emergency preparedness. The review identified five core components of resilience for health security: physical and psychological health of the population, social and economic well-being of the community, effective risk communication, integration and involvement of organizations (both government and nongovernmental), and social connectedness.[1] These components are reflected in the definition of community resilience that we present in the next chapter. Additional information about the literature review methodology is presented in Appendix A.

**Stakeholder Focus Groups**

Between January and April 2010, we conducted six focus groups with key stakeholders to obtain feedback on a draft definition of community resilience and to identify activities to build resilience and inform the measurement of community resilience. The goal of the focus groups was to obtain community stakeholder input on what constitutes community resilience in the context of national health security, to identify what key activities would build or enhance resilience in this context, and to describe ways to measure reaching the objective of resilience. Five of the meetings were held in person in the following locations: New Orleans, Los Angeles, Washington, D.C., Chicago, and Miami. The sixth focus group was conducted virtually using a web-based seminar format and consisted of attendees of the previous focus groups. The locations of the focus groups were selected to represent geographic diversity. We acknowledge that the settings for the focus groups were in major U.S. cities (see "Key Limitations to Consider"); however, there were logistic reasons to select settings in which the research team has some local partnerships with which to organize the groups. We purposefully selected a focus group composition that represented the range of government and nongovernmental stakeholders who are responsible in some way for enhancing national health security. As such, the focus groups included representatives from state and local government (emergency management, homeland security, health, social services, disaster organizations); universities; and such nongovernmental organizations (NGOs) as volunteer organizations, faith-based organizations, schools, national NGOs, and other community organizations. These discussions did not include employers or other for-profit business, which we reference as a limitation of this study. We worked with local health departments and local emergency planning committees to identify potential participants and then reviewed the list to make sure that we invited people who represented each of the categories (i.e., at least one person from each area) listed earlier. Each focus group lasted 1.5 to 2 hours, and followed a semistructured protocol.

The focus groups were designed so that each group discussion built on previous discussions, allowing us to continually review and refine the definition and suggested activities from prior groups. Early groups focused on defining what constitutes a resilient community and soliciting activities for building resilience. Later groups also addressed these topics and discussed specific aspects of the activities, including the appropriate lead organization for each activity and measurement of each activity's impact on community resilience.

**Other Meetings with Subject Matter Experts**

We conducted three meetings with SMEs, including federal representatives, researchers, and health department leaders, to solicit additional comments on the draft definition of community resilience. It was important to include federal and local health department perspectives,

---

[1]   Detailed results of this literature review and explanation for the framework are summarized in Chandra et al., 2010.

given their roles in implementing the NHSS. The researchers were able to provide input based on lessons learned from prior disasters, including case study analyses and other studies that could inform the definition. The subject matter experts included representatives from federal agencies involved with developing the NHSS, such as DHS, the U.S. Department of Housing and Urban Development, and agencies within HHS. Researchers were included who had published extensively on the topic of community resilience or related areas, such as community empowerment or engagement. Additional health department leaders were included who had been part of earlier regional meetings to develop the NHSS but had not been included in the local focus groups for this study. The SME groups also provided input on draft measures related to community resilience for the NHSS Biennial Implementation Plan, primarily those focused on Objective 1 (fostering informed and empowered individuals and communities) and Objective 8 (enhancing post-incident health recovery).

**Integration of Information**

The RAND research team integrated the data from all three data collection efforts to develop the final definition and to determine the most critical or commonly identified community resilience–building activities (i.e., those that emerged in at least two group discussions). The definition was also reviewed by an HHS-wide workgroup. In developing the final activity list, the RAND team removed activities that were not consistently referenced by focus groups (i.e., eliminating items mentioned by only a single respondent) or that did not have a rationale guided by the literature review. In an effort to organize and streamline the list, the research team flagged activities that were duplicative and, where possible, combined activities that had similar or overlapping themes or intentions. However, the team did not reduce the list further, given that there are no established criteria for evaluating the potential impact, effectiveness, or relative priority of the activities for enhancing community resilience. Further, the team preserved the wording of the activities as articulated by participants, to the extent possible.

**Key Limitations to Consider**

There are a few limitations to consider in reviewing this report. First, the activities in this report reflect only those identified in focus group and SME discussions. Thus, the fact that we did not have a focus group site in a rural setting should be considered when reviewing the appropriateness of the suggested activities. Despite concerted effort, our groups did not include membership by the business community. Further, resilience plan development should include the perspectives of the for-profit sector, given its role in returning a community to routine functioning after disaster. Second, aside from the process described in the prior paragraph, the list of activities was not subject to additional vetting based on feasibility or the sociopolitical context in which activities may be implemented. Subsequent analytic steps should include community review and testing of activities to further refine and organize the list. It will be important for communities (see the next section) to use the roadmap as a starting point for local community resilience strategy development. Third, none of these activities has undergone rigorous evaluation. Before a community resilience *toolkit* can be developed, communities will need to use this roadmap, report on lessons learned, and assess the impact of implementing particular activities.

## Using This Report

As described previously, this report is intended to be a roadmap to guide local planning. Thus, community-planning teams (perhaps led by the local health department) should review the content of the report with attention to the extent to which they are using the levers (or tools) to improve community resilience. A suggested approach to using this report is provided in the checklist below:

√   Review the core components and levers of community resilience (see Chapter Two). Consider the ways that your community is using each lever to reach the core component. For example, in what ways is the community engaging (lever = engagement) community stakeholders to improve the component of *risk communication*?

√   Read through the individual lever chapters (Chapters Three through Ten). *Ask yourself, in what ways is my community meeting the critical elements of each lever?*

√   Depending on your answer to the above questions, read the activities that correspond to the lever(s) of interest. *Is your community doing any of these activities, or could your community expand or strengthen efforts in these areas? Ask yourself, what activities can my community pursue alone, and where will my community need state and/or federal partnership?* Each activity provides a brief rationale, suggested leaders, and possible steps for implementation. The goal is not to conduct every activity for every element. Rather, communities should select activities based on their needs and assets.

√   Use the roadmap to develop a local plan for your community with activities for building or enhancing resilience. Consider whether the activities are feasible, and where you can leverage existing resources to complete them. The goal is not to complete all of the activities in this roadmap but to select the ones that make sense for your community.

# CHAPTER TWO

# Definition and Application of Community Resilience

This chapter provides a foundation for the remainder of the report by presenting the definition of community resilience that resulted from the literature review, focus groups, and meetings with SMEs, along with a conceptual framework for organizing the activities for building community resilience presented in subsequent chapters.

## Definition of Community Resilience in the Context of National Health Security

### Process for Developing the Definition

In order to develop a definition of community resilience, we created an inventory of the definitions of community resilience in the literature (see Appendix B). The definitions were included in articles from diverse disciplinary backgrounds, including disaster sciences, psychology, and sociology. The findings from the literature review were also used to identify the core components of community resilience in the context of national health security, which are shown in Figure 2.1.

**Figure 2.1**
**Core Components of Community Resilience in the Context of National Health Security**

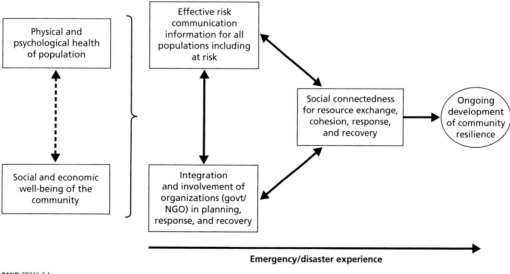

RAND *TR915-2.1*

The definition draws upon both the literature review as well as discussions with focus group participants. Participants from across all focus groups suggested that the following common features would be evident in a resilient community:

- Engagement at the community level, including a sense of cohesiveness and neighborhood involvement or integration
- Partnership among organizations, including integrated pre-event planning, exercises, and agreements
- Sustained local leadership supported by partnership with state and federal government
- Effective and culturally relevant education about risks
- Optimal community health and access to quality health services
- Integration of preparedness and wellness
- Rapid restoration of services and social networks
- Individual-level preparedness and self-sufficiency
- Targeted strategies that empower and engage vulnerable populations
- Financial resiliency of families and businesses, and efficient leveraging of resources for recovery.

Based on the literature review and discussions with these participants, we developed a definition of community resilience in the context of national health security.

We acknowledge that the definition of "community" can widely vary; it can be a geographic term or can be bounded by membership to a cultural group. Although it will be important for local planning teams to define community boundaries with community stakeholders, for the purpose of this roadmap, we primarily use a geographic definition guided by the catchment area of the local health department (e.g., city/county/parish/municipality).

### Definition of Community Resilience

The definition of community resilience is shown in the box. The definition draws upon both the literature review (Norris, 2008; Chandra et al., 2010; HHS, 2009; HHS, 2010a), as well as discussions with focus group participants. The definition is included in the draft NHSS Biennial Implementation Plan (HHS, 2010b).

## Application of the Definition: Levers

### Process for Identifying Levers

Although Figure 2.1 provides a useful way to organize findings from the literature review and focus groups in order to generate the community resilience definition, the framework was not as immediately useful for identifying community-level activities that build resilience. Further, it did not provide a framework for testing the impact of these activities at the community level.

Thus, in order to identify key activities for building and strengthening community resilience, we drew on additional findings from the literature review, focus groups, and SME meetings to define eight "levers" (see rounded boxes in Figure 2.2) that can be used by communities to build on existing efforts and strengthen community resilience in the context of the health security (e.g., wellness, engagement). To identify the levers, we developed a coding scheme on which to compare the activities identified in the focus groups and consultations with subject

---

**Definition of Community Resilience**

**Main Definition:**
*Community resilience entails the ongoing and developing capacity of the community to account for its vulnerabilities and develop capabilities that aid that community in (1) preventing, withstanding, and mitigating the stress of a health incident; (2) recovering in a way that restores the community to a state of self-sufficiency and at least the same level of health and social functioning after a health incident; and (3) using knowledge from a past response to strengthen the community's ability to withstand the next health incident.*

**Key Components:**
Key components or "building blocks" of community resilience that affect both a community's pre-event vulnerability to disaster and its adaptive capacity to recover include the physical and psychological health of the population; social and economic well-being; individual, family, and community knowledge and attitudes regarding self-reliance and self-help; effective risk communication; level of social integration of government and nongovernmental organizations in planning, response, and recovery; and the social connectedness of community members. In order to build community resilience, a community must develop capabilities in the following areas: active engagement of community stakeholders in health event planning and personal preparedness, development of social networks, creation of health-promoting opportunities to improve the physical and psychological health of the community (as well as to address disparities in health across subgroups), plans and programs that address and support the functional needs of at-risk individuals (including children), institution of plans to respond effectively to the post-disaster physical and psychological health needs of community members, and rebuilding plans for health and social systems that can be activated immediately.

---

matter experts. The coding scheme is based on the common themes found in the resilience–building activity descriptions (summarized in the rest of this report), the components of Figure 2.1 that were derived from the literature review and focus groups, and the elements of a resilient community identified from the focus groups. Study team members then reviewed notes from literature analysis, focus groups, and activity lists to categorize each resilience-building activity according to one or more levers. If an activity was coded for more than one lever, team members discussed the rationale and came to consensus about the final assignment or placement. In addition, some codes or levers were combined because the distinction between levers could not be supported by literature or a unique theme from focus group discussion.

**Levers for Building Community Resilience**

Figure 2.2 displays the eight levers we describe in this report (in rounded boxes). The levers build on the core components in Figure 2.1, but expand that organization into an applied framework. These levers strengthen the five components (in rectangular boxes) that are correlated with community resilience in the specific context of enhancing health security or public health preparedness. **Wellness** and **access** contribute to the development of the social and economic well-being of a community and the physical and psychological health of the population. Specific to the disaster experience, **education** can be used to improve effective risk communication, **engagement** and **self-sufficiency** are needed to build social connectedness, and **partnership** helps ensure governmental and nongovernmental organizations are integrated. **Quality** and **efficiency** are ongoing levers that cut across all levers and core components of community resilience. Thus, considerations about quality monitoring and resource efficiency are essential in developing local community resilience–building plans.

As activities related to the levers strengthen each of the components of community resilience, a community moves closer to achieving community resilience (shown in the circle) because developing resilience is not static but rather is an iterative and ongoing process.

Figure 2.2 provides the conceptual framework for the next eight chapters, each of which focuses on one lever for building resilience.

**Figure 2.2**
**Levers and Core Components of Community Resilience**

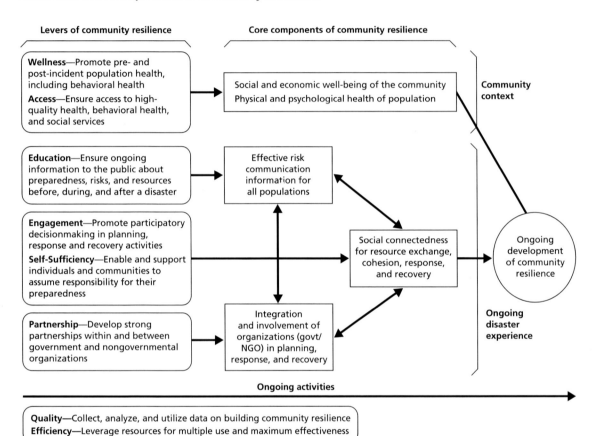

RAND TR915-2.2

# Wellness: Promote Population Health Before and After an Incident, Including Behavioral Health

The extent to which a community and its resources are affected by a health incident depends in part on the existing wellness levels of community members—their physical, behavioral, and social well-being at the time the incident occurs. Because collective well-being before a health incident can affect people's need for resources and the length of the recovery period, sustaining an overall level of wellness can serve as a social and individual resource for resilience (Norris et al., 2008; Pfefferbaum et al., 2008). The overall resilience of a community can rest on the extent to which community members practice healthy lifestyles and are aware of the community's health-related functional needs (e.g., number of people who need transportation assistance, number of people on dialysis) that, if ignored, can render emergency response and recovery difficult. Communities that are already healthy (e.g., have a lower prevalence of chronic disease) are better able to withstand the trauma of a health incident (Aldrich & Benson, 2008), and will generally require less medical support before, during, and after a health incident (Kailes & Enders, 2007; Ku & Matani, 2001). Conversely, recovery may be more difficult for at-risk individuals and communities that have a lower level of wellness—in other words, for those with fewer resources to cope with or mitigate the impact of a health incident (Andrulis, Siddiqui, & Gantner, 2007; Fothergill, Maestas, & Darlington, 1999). All this suggests the need to address existing health conditions as well as population vulnerabilities (National Council on Disability, 2005), with special consideration given to at-risk populations, i.e., individuals with functional needs (Brodie et al., 2006; Norris et al., 2008).

One way to support pre-incident prevention and population wellness is to create a culture in which individuals understand the relationship between individual and community preparedness, and know how to remain generally healthy (Norris et al., 2008; Pfefferbaum et al., 2008). Fostering such a culture may depend in part on appropriately conveying information to the public. Messaging that is appropriately framed may motivate people to take actions to improve their own physical and psychological health (Benight et al., 1999). Properly framed messages can also help the community maintain psychological health by supporting a positive focus on prevention and health and wellness rather than stoking fears. Messages need to be culturally appropriate because cultural barriers (e.g., language gaps, differing social norms) can be a major source of misunderstanding of health information (Ng, 2005). In particular, the extent to which people—especially in at-risk populations—are influenced by the framing of wellness messages and prevention efforts may differ by culture and ethnic group (Walker & Chestnut, 2003).

Key elements of community wellness are shown in Table 3.1.

**Table 3.1**
**Key Elements of Community Wellness**

| Element | Description | Activities for State and Local Entities |
|---|---|---|
| 1. Promote public understanding of health and wellness. | Community members understand how to prevent or mitigate the impact of health threats by maintaining health and wellness on an ongoing basis. As described in Figure 2.1, resilience rests on a foundation of community wellness, so communities must embrace a guiding orientation toward health promotion and overall well-being. | Train workforce on culturally competent and linguistically appropriate healthcare. Develop public health messaging to promote healthy lifestyles and bolster psychological wellness, particularly coping skills and resilience attitudes. |
| 2. Ensure sufficient community health resources, along with the capability to leverage those resources to achieve desired outcomes. | Communities have appropriate resources to address physical and psychological health, and the functional needs of at-risk individuals. The ability to leverage these resources depends in part on knowledge about how to allocate them. | Conduct an annual assessment of population health vulnerabilities. Ensure pre–health incident access to health services and post–health incident continuity of care. Ensure that the population receives timely and age-appropriate vaccinations. |

## Activities Related to Community Wellness

Suggested activities that communities can take to support each of these elements are discussed in detail below. Note that each element has suggested activities based on the literature review and focus group data collection. Communities should consider which activities will meet their needs and build on existing efforts. Activities that are underway should be evaluated, and lessons learned shared with other communities. See Appendix C for an example community prioritization tool that can be used with this roadmap. The activities within each element are grouped by the level of implementation—state/local, then federal/national. In Table 3.1, we list the activities specific to state and local entities given that much of the resilience-building efforts occur at these levels. Some activities are shared by government and nongovernmental entities. For each activity, we briefly describe a rationale, the leaders, and potential steps for implementation.

### Element 1: Activities to Promote Public Understanding of Health and Wellness

The activities in this element include (1) training the workforce on culturally competent and linguistically appropriate healthcare and (2) developing public health messaging.

**Train workforce on culturally competent and linguistically appropriate healthcare.**

*Rationale:* Different cultures perceive and respond to traumatic events differently. Some culturally or linguistically isolated populations (racial and ethnic minorities, immigrants, rural populations) may misunderstand public health information, e.g., by underestimating risk (Andrulis et al., 2007; Carter-Pokras et al., 2007; Chen et al., 2007; Fothergill, Maestas, & Darlington, 1999; Shiu-Thornton et al., 2007).

*Key leaders:* State and local government and nongovernmental organizations.

*Potential steps:* Public health agencies and organizations at the state and local levels should train health and social service providers to deliver care—both routinely and in case of disaster—in a way that is culturally competent and linguistically accessible to different cultural groups.

**Develop public health messaging to promote healthy lifestyles and bolster psychological wellness, particularly coping skills and resilience attitudes.**

*Rationale:* Health incidents unleash many potential stressors, such as casualties, displacement, and loss of property or financial resources. These stressors can deplete coping resources, threatening individuals' psychological well-being and their ability to function effectively. However, individuals' available coping resources function as a buffer against psychological distress.

*Key leaders:* Federal and state government and national nongovernmental organizations.

*Potential steps:* Public messages should be designed to provide routine information about preventive steps community members can take to ensure healthy living and support psychological wellness. Such messages could include

- positive framing of public health messages—e.g., emphasizing health benefits and general wellness may be more effective than fear-based preparedness messaging, which individuals may tend to avoid
- content that is culturally appropriate for diverse populations, which should increase the likelihood that the information is understood, particularly for at-risk populations.

### Element 2: Activities to Ensure Sufficient Community Health Resources, Along with the Capability to Leverage Those Resources to Achieve Desired Outcomes

The activities in this element include (1) regularly assessing population health, (2) ensuring access to health services, and (3) ensuring vaccinations.

**Conduct an annual assessment of population health vulnerabilities.**

*Rationale:* To facilitate health services that promote wellness, population vulnerabilities, such as individuals' chronic conditions, must be well understood. Routinely analyzing and characterizing the preexisting health status of a community offers critical information to guide pre-event resource allocation and also has implications for recovery planning.

*Key leaders:* State and local government.

*Potential steps:* To conduct such an assessment, various approaches could be considered:

- State governments should be engaged annually to assess common vulnerabilities among the population that would limit its ability to absorb the stress of a disaster.
- Local health departments could share the results of ongoing health monitoring with state government and community organizations. These assessments could be conducted in conjunction with other community resilience–building activities, such as identifying geographic concentrations of at-risk individuals.
- The community health risk profile template being developed for the NHSS Biennial Implementation Plan could be used to conduct a community vulnerability assessment.

**Ensure pre–health incident access to health services, as well as post–health incident continuity of care.**

*Rationale:* Routine access to preventive healthcare is important for population wellness. Communities having a greater proportion of residents with chronic conditions, such as obesity, kidney disease requiring ongoing dialysis, or other conditions requiring durable medical equipment, will generally need more medical support before, during, and after a disaster.

*Key leaders:* Federal and local government agencies.

*Potential steps:* To ensure that community members have health insurance and access to health services:

- Health and emergency response systems should be sustained as well as strengthened, both to prevent health incidents from occurring and to minimize severity of incidents that have occurred.
- Health services must be accessible to help communities recover after a health incident.
- Regional healthcare coalitions may be built to ensure that health systems have adequate capacity during response and recovery.

### Ensure that the population receives timely and age-appropriate vaccinations.

*Rationale:* Greater numbers of vaccinated individuals translate to lower likelihood of disease transmission throughout the population. Furthermore, a vaccinated population is a healthier population (i.e., more equipped to withstand the physical stressors of an incident) (Weycker et al., 2005; Nichols, 1998). A vaccinated population may also be more likely to accept novel vaccines in case of new health threats.

*Key leaders:* Federal and state government, local nongovernmental organizations.

*Potential steps:* To ensure access to existing vaccines—both routinely and after disasters:

- The federal government could partner with state governments to develop a robust distribution plan for vaccines.
- State governments could work closely with local NGOs, as well as pharmacies, schools, and other entities that can serve as sites for clinics.
- National and local media could be engaged to ensure an effective communication strategy that informs the public about the importance, availability, and safety of vaccines.

# CHAPTER FOUR

# Access: Ensure Access to High-Quality Health, Behavioral Health, and Social Resources and Services

Vulnerable or poorer households and communities tend to recover slowly after a health incident. Their already low levels of resilience may be exacerbated by lack of access to adequate resources and services. For instance, in rural communities, scarce resources due to poverty and geographic dispersion mean that, in the aftermath of a disaster, local public health departments, rural health centers, and other organizations may be stretched too thin or be inadequately equipped to handle the unique needs of their community (Dobalian et al., 2007). Access to high-quality resources and services—such as serviceable infrastructure—is an important part of community resilience, particularly for vulnerable populations.

Key elements of access to high-quality health, behavioral health, and social resources and services are shown in Table 4.1.

**Table 4.1**
**Key Elements of High-Quality Health, Behavioral Health, and Social Resources and Services**

| Element | Description | Activities for State and Local Entities |
|---|---|---|
| 1. Ensure continuity of healthcare and related social services. | Federal and state governments identify local NGOs with the capacity and capability to meet the health, behavioral health, and social service needs of constituents rapidly, effectively, and uniformly. | Ensure continuity of care for those needing long-term medical/health services post-disaster. |
| 2. Facilitate transition to recovery planning. | Plans are developed to assess community needs for resources at the onset, during and after a health incident. | Identify existing community assets that can play a role in preparedness through recovery. |
| 3. Provide health services and remove barriers to accessing them. | Rapid dissemination and implementation of services and interventions is critical. For example, traumatized disaster survivors may require psychological orientation to function and begin to recover in other ways. Cultural barriers may prevent some individuals from complying with public health recommendations. | Provide "psychological first aid" or other early psychological or behavioral health interventions after a disaster. Bridge cultural differences to increase understanding of and cooperation with public health recommendations. |

## Activities Related to Access to High-Quality Health, Behavioral Health, and Social Resources and Services

Suggested activities relating to each of these elements in Table 4.1 are discussed in detail below.

### Element 1: Activities to Ensure Continuity of Healthcare and Related Social Services

The suggested activity in this element describes ensuring continuity of care.

**Ensure continuity of care for those needing long-term medical/health services post-disaster.**

*Rationale:* Individuals with health vulnerabilities may have high levels of medical need throughout all stages of disaster, including long-term recovery (Kailes & Enders, 2007; Ku & Matani, 2001). Addressing the many needs for preparedness, response, and recovery activities requires routine, seamless coordination among government and NGO partners as responsibility shifts among the different lead entities.

*Key leaders:* Federal/state/local governments, local nongovernmental organizations.

*Potential steps:* Governments at each level could work with local NGOs to provide a smooth transition of responsibility among stakeholders to ensure the delivery of long-term health services to at-risk individuals.

### Element 2: Activities to Facilitate Transition to Recovery Planning

The activities in this element include (1) identifying existing community assets and (2) planning for low-income populations.

**Identify existing community assets (e.g., fire stations, businesses, faith-based organizations) that can play a role in preparedness through recovery.**

*Rationale:* Populations are vulnerable in a public health incident if they have difficulty accessing or using resources that are offered as part of preparedness, recovery, and response plans (Dobalian et al., 2007). Communities often have a wide array of social and physical assets that local governments and NGOs can leverage in creative ways during the response and recovery stages.

*Key leaders*: Local government and local nongovernmental organizations.

*Potential steps:* Governments and community-based organizations could routinely work in partnership to identify innovative uses of traditional resources currently available within communities, using local knowledge of the community's characteristics to enhance the effectiveness of response and recovery efforts.

**Plan for longer-term food, shelter, clothing, and medical needs of recovering low-income populations.**

*Rationale:* Appropriate planning for long-term recovery from disaster helps restore the health and livelihood of low-income individuals. In addition, adequate support helps rebuild and even improve community resilience, thus mitigating vulnerability to future disasters. Since low-income individuals are disproportionately affected by disaster (Dobalian et al., 2007; Morrow, 1999; Norris et al., 2008), it is important to consider these impacts when estimating needed support.

*Key leaders:* Federal/state government.

*Potential steps:* Effective planning for post-health incident housing, for example, could include the following:

- Provide flexible options to meet the community's immediate needs for shelter while incorporating long-term efforts to restoring affordable housing for affected communities.
- Routinely revisit and update policies that guide funding and implementation of post-health incident housing programs, ensuring that solutions are timely and cost-effective, while offering maximum flexibility to affected community members.
- Give attention to individuals and families with low incomes, who often cannot qualify for needed loans that would help them return to their homes more quickly or obtain new housing.

**Element 3: Activities to Provide Health Services and Remove Barriers to Accessing Them**
The activities in this element include (1) providing psychological interventions and (2) addressing cultural barriers to understanding public health recommendations.

**Provide "psychological first aid" or other early psychological or behavioral health interventions after disaster.**

*Rationale:* Early psychological and behavioral health interventions after disasters, such as "psychological first aid," are important in rebuilding coping resources (National Child Traumatic Stress Network, 2011; Ursano et al., 2007).

*Key leaders:* Federal/state/local governments, local nongovernmental organizations.

*Potential steps:* All levels of government should work in partnership with local NGOs to do the following:

- Ensure that psychological first aid and other resources are provided to disaster victims as quickly as possible in order to reduce psychological distress.
- Educate community members about appropriate social or emotional support that they might offer to friends or neighbors experiencing stress.
- Incorporate ongoing evaluation of these interventions during future disaster responses, given that the evidence base is currently limited with respect to these types of behavioral health interventions.

**Bridge cultural differences to increase understanding of and cooperation with public health recommendations.**

*Rationale:* Cultural differences may lead to misunderstandings about the nature and availability of recovery resources, or lead to mistrust between response agency workers and minority persons (Cutter et al., 2003; Morrow, 1999). Specifically, some populations (racial and ethnic minorities, immigrants, rural populations) may mistrust government/public agencies (see, e.g., Blanchard et al., 2005; Brodie et al., 2006; Cordasco et al., 2007) and tend not to rely on such sources for information (Carter-Pokras et al., 2007; Chen et al., 2007).

*Key leaders:* Federal/state/local governments, local nongovernmental organizations.

*Potential steps*: Communities should ensure that these populations have routine access to all services by striving to make information accessible to all its members, including at-risk populations. This could include the following:

- Government could partner with institutions serving culturally diverse populations to recruit a diverse workforce to health security–related fields. In doing so, cooperation and compliance with public health recommendations should increase, and a greater range of health services should be accessible to vulnerable populations.

- Government agencies—in the short-term—could conduct community-level focus groups, town hall–type meetings, or engage community leaders in message development to capture various cultural perspectives.

# CHAPTER FIVE

# Education: Ensure Ongoing Information to the Public About Preparedness, Risks, and Resources Before, During, and After a Disaster

Community education is an ongoing process in which the community acquires knowledge about roles, responsibilities, and expectations for individual preparedness as well as the ways in which individuals can work collectively with other community members to respond to and recover from a health incident. Public health education is an important lever for ensuring that individuals and communities are educated about health security risks and know how to prepare, respond, and recover. Community education also means that individuals know where to turn for help both for themselves and their neighbors, enabling the entire community to be resilient in the face of a disaster.

Effective risk communication is critical to ensuring ongoing regular information exchange with the public. Risk communication is broadly defined as the interactive process that involves the exchange of information between parties about a sensitive issue (Committee on Risk Perception and Communication & National Research Council, 1989). Key components of risk communication include the "message" that is being conveyed, the "messenger" who delivers the message, and the medium through which the message is delivered. According to Andrulis, Siddiqui, a& Gantner (2007), effective risk communication means selecting messages, messengers, and strategies for delivery that succeed in disseminating risk information across the stages of a disaster. Effective risk communication is essential to resilience because it provides accurate information about dangers and behavioral options for mitigation. It increases knowledge and therefore bolsters a community's adaptive capacity. In addition, effective risk communication builds trust and overcomes distrust, which can have important consequences for mental health, likely adherence to government recommendations, and social cohesion (Norris et al., 2008). The content and availability of risk information and related materials are vital for increasing a community's self-efficacy before and during an event.

Training community partners, businesses, and other lead agencies in preparedness and in the best ways to communicate with community members also creates a stronger social infrastructure for resilience. Strong communication networks allow for a cohesive, integrated, and engaged community population. Targeted strategies help reach at-risk and other populations. Communication networks that integrate the wisdom of healthcare providers (e.g., physicians, emergency responders), health officials, representatives from diverse public groups, and trusted citizen representatives make for stronger and coordinated community education (Schoch-Spana, 2008).

Lastly, population health literacy is a distinct component of community resilience. There are three dimensions to health literacy: the basic knowledge needed to understand and take action on health issues (conceptual foundations), the skills necessary to make public health decisions that benefit the community (critical skills), and the skills and resources necessary to address health concerns through civic engagement (civic orientation) (Freedman et al., 2009). Low health literacy influences not only how individuals receive and process messages but also how they navigate complex disaster settings and the recovery environment. High health literacy in the community can support the community's ability to process messages, take action, and plan for recovery.

Key elements of community education are shown in Table 5.1.

## Activities Related to Community Education

Suggested activities relating to each of these elements are discussed in detail below.

### Element 1: Activities to Bolster Community Resilience by Providing Accurate Information About Health Threats

These activities entail developing appropriate risk communication messages, particularly ones that focus on pre-disaster planning and emphasize the importance of preventive care.

**Communicate realistic recovery timeline and plan to set reasonable expectations, given likely post-event challenges.**

**Table 5.1**
**Key Elements of Community Education**

| Element | Description | Activities for State and Local Entities |
| --- | --- | --- |
| 1. Use effective risk communication to bolster community resilience by providing accurate information about health threats. | Communication strategies and content should acknowledge the individual and cultural beliefs and community norms that shape expectations of what is to be done before, during, and after event. | Communicate realistic recovery timeline/plan to set reasonable expectations, given likely post-event challenges. Develop and disseminate messages that improve understanding between individual and community health. |
| 2. Work collectively to train and educate partner agencies and to have an effective and coordinated communication system or network. | Strong communication networks are critical for resilience. These networks should rely on diversity of mode and content as well as ability to link social networks effectively. | Support and promote the use of social media among communities and organizations. Proactively educate media organizations regarding their role in facilitating health incident response. Train community partners and lay health advisors in proper risk communication techniques. |
| 3. Build basic health literacy and awareness of health issues. | The underlying literacy of the community, particularly health literacy, supports its ability to process messages, take action, and plan for recovery. | Promote healthy lifestyles by ensuring that the population has information about health promotion and disease prevention. Bolster coping skills and psychological wellness by developing public health campaigns focused on these messages. |

*Rationale:* Community members who expect recovery to be swift and unchallenging may be vulnerable to greater mental health effects in the post-event phase because of disappointment and frustration. Recovery is challenging and involves many distinct processes—for example, post-incident health recovery entails reconnecting families and community members, rebuilding health system infrastructure, providing psychological first aid and case management, and restoring social networks (HHS, 2010a).

*Key leaders:* State and local government and NGOs.

*Potential steps:* Once recovery planning has occurred and realistic timelines established, NGOs and government should communicate key dates and provide progress reports to community members in order to ensure accountability.

**Develop and disseminate messages that improve understanding between individual and community health.**

*Rationale:* Resilient communities are composed of individuals who understand the interdependent relationship between individual and community health.

*Key leaders:* Federal, state, and local government; NGOs.

*Potential steps:* Framing messages to emphasize the connections between individual and community helps to motivate community members to take preparedness measures. Governments and NGOs should develop these positive messages related to the relationship between individual and community health and should test them to ensure that they resonate with community members and promote the value of individual and civic responsibility for a community's well-being. These organizations should disseminate such messages broadly to community members in a variety of formats (e.g., radio, newspaper, TV). To encourage this messaging, federal, state, and local governments should work together to determine what incentives (e.g., funding, other) could be used to motivate this movement toward community preparedness. The federal government can help by providing templates to help communities promote preparedness and strengthen local resilience.

**Create health-related risk communication messages for the general public that adhere to general principles and best practices in risk communication.**

*Rationale:* Effective risk communication bolsters community resilience by providing accurate information about health threats and increasing knowledge about protective behaviors and support resources, thereby bolstering a community's capacity to adapt, especially during a health incident.

*Key leaders:* Federal government, and state and local public health departments.

*Potential steps:* Officials at federal and state level can take proactive steps to facilitate the timely development and dissemination of high-quality health-related messages during an emergency. In nonemergency times, state and local governments should consider community norms and the range of individual beliefs in crafting health-related risk communication messages to ensure that messages address citizens' expectations and social context, and promote dialogue among community members on the best use of resources.

**Tailor information for at-risk individuals with consideration to issues of health literacy; culture; trusted spokespersons/channels; preferred languages; and preferred, alternate, and accessible formats.**

*Rationale:* In a resilient community, key messages can be accessed and understood by the entire community, allowing all populations to benefit equally from relevant information. As described in the NHSS, effective health-related risk communication involves reaching all segments of the affected population in ways they trust and understand (HHS, 2009).

*Key leaders:* Federal government, state and local public health departments; national and local NGOs.

*Potential steps:* To communicate effectively, health departments and other government organizations must understand how to tailor communication to specific members of the community. Local government and local NGOs should conduct formative research (e.g., community forums) to identify key populations, their information needs, effective media channels (including use of social media such as Facebook and Twitter), and trusted spokespersons. Federal and state governments should then develop tailored risk communication strategies for delivering targeted messages to specific populations.

Other strategies to communicate effectively with at-risk individuals include the following:

- Take into account community norms and the range of individual beliefs in crafting risk communication messages; address citizens' expectations and social context, and promote dialogue among community members on the best use of resources (Paton et al., 2008).
- Work with employers and NGO partners to identify trusted sources of information and help encourage public involvement and open communication during a crisis (Paton et al., 2008).
- Identify and train community-based messengers in the principles of risk communication and use them to deliver important public health messages during a crisis (Shiu-Thornton et al., 2007).
- Build trust in advance of a disaster through community partnerships, lay health advisor training, and use of appropriate channels for delivering risk information (Quinn, 2008).

### Element 2: Activities to Train and Educate Partner Agencies and to Develop an Effective and Coordinated Communication System or Network

This activities focus on training and developing a comprehensive and robust communication network.

**Support and promote the use of social media among communities and organizations.**

*Rationale:* Risk communication and other public health messages are most effective when they are delivered through trusted channels that are understandable and culturally appropriate. A broad range of strategies is necessary to reach all populations, including the newest forms of communication.

*Key leaders:* Local government and local NGOs.

*Potential steps:* Local government and local NGOs should conduct formative research (e.g., community forums) to identify key populations for whom new media (including use of social media such as Facebook and Twitter) are the most effective communication channels. Federal and state governments should then develop tailored risk communication strategies to deliver targeted messages to these populations through these media.

**Proactively educate media organizations regarding their role in facilitating health incident response and not exacerbating that response with sensational reporting.**

*Rationale:* Sensational reporting about health incidents can overwhelm community members, and repeated coverage of distressing events can traumatize individuals outside the affected community (e.g., family members and friends) or revictimize individuals from within the affected area.

*Key leaders:* Community-based organizations and the media.

*Potential steps:* Community-based organizations should reach out to local media outlets and encourage them to provide educational information to the public on mitigating potential health threats. Media can be an ally during a disaster by educating the community about actions they can take to ensure their safety and to minimize the impact of the disaster on their community. These organizations can work with media to ensure that truly representative stories are depicted during and after disaster and that accurate information is reaching all residents.

**Involve advocacy organizations, service entities, and support groups representing at-risk individuals in the design and dissemination of health-related information.**

*Rationale:* At-risk individuals are more receptive to health-related risk communication messages when these are crafted to fit with relevant cultural norms and come from trusted sources.

*Key leaders:* State and local government; local NGOs.

*Potential steps:* Government health officials enhance the level of trust in messaging among community members by taking a participatory approach with local organizations to disseminate health-related information and empowering organizations to develop preparedness materials. Local organizations should not passively receive materials from government; rather, they can take ownership of messages by tailoring language and creating preparedness materials that are better accepted by the populations they serve.

**Train community partners and lay health advisors in proper risk communication techniques and engage them as information disseminators during an event.**

*Rationale:* Resilient communities are those in which all segments of the population are likely to act on official messages, and this messaging can result in behavior change. Thus, it is essential that risk communication and public education strategies related to public health and medical issues establish trust among community members, thereby improving adherence to government recommendations.

*Key leaders:* Federal, state, and local government; local NGOs, employers, faith-based groups, schools.

*Potential steps:* Governments should attempt to build trust in advance of a disaster. Partners might include established organizations (e.g., Neighborhood Watch), employers, faith-based groups, and schools to educate and encourage youth to communicate messages to their families. To accomplish this, local governments should work with employers and NGO partners to identify trusted sources of public health and medical information and help encourage public involvement and open communication during a crisis. Local governments, employers, and NGO local partners should also identify and train community-based messengers, such as health promoter/promatoras and medical interpreters, in the principles of risk communication and use them to deliver important public health messages during a crisis and to disseminate research about what works.

**Ensure that the community has a functional communications infrastructure and regionalized communications network that links health professionals, including medical providers, health officials, diverse publics, and volunteers to ensure timeliness, quality, and consistency of messaging.**

*Rationale:* Communications infrastructure facilitates the flow of risk information to large segments of a community, improving awareness of recommended countermeasures and responses and ensuring consistency of messaging. A functional infrastructure includes a regional communications center and network. It also includes battery-operated internal and external systems readily available in case of a power outage. The infrastructure should employ appropriate technologies to support these networks (e.g., web portals, robust cell towers, GPS) that can quickly reconnect families and other social structures.

*Key leaders:* State and local government.

*Potential steps:* State and local governments should take steps before a disaster to leverage strong relationships among response organizations. This requires engaging all relevant stakeholders and bringing them together to clearly define roles and responsibilities, gain a better understanding of each organization's mission and perspective, and develop a set of common goals. States should ensure that communications networks incorporate input from multiple public officials and medical providers by integrating information from physicians, emergency responders, health department officials, and citizen representatives who have appropriate risk communication training. Information provided to the public needs to be coordinated and consistent across all response organizations.

### Element 3: Activities to Build Basic Health Literacy and Awareness of Health Issues

These activities focus on building a community's health literacy, particularly during nonemergent times (or periods not focused on disaster response).

**Promote healthy lifestyles by ensuring that the population has information about health promotion and disease prevention.**

*Rationale:* All stakeholders in local communities should take steps to promote the health of community members.

*Key leaders:* State and local public health; federal and local NGOs.

*Potential steps:* To promote health of community members, provide more comprehensive health education and investment in health promotion activities, including programs that improve the underlying health literacy of a population. This includes identifying creative ways to teach community members about health, how to access resources, and how to read and interpret health information. This education can be integrated into school and community group activities. During an incident, individuals with high health literacy are more likely to be able to access, interpret, and act upon official health-related messages and navigate health services in the complex response-and-recovery environment.

**Bolster coping skills and psychological wellness by developing public health campaigns focused on these messages.**

*Rationale:* For a community to withstand and recover from a disaster, it is critical that individuals have adequate coping resources. Psychological wellness can be improved by educating the public with accurate and timely information on coping options.

*Key leaders:* Local governments and NGOs.

***Potential steps:*** Local governments and NGOs should disseminate information to the public about stress management that allows individuals to address stressors more easily, thereby lessening psychological distress. Further, these organizations can lead efforts to implement evidence-based psychological wellness and stress management programs.

# CHAPTER SIX

# Engagement: Promote Participatory Decisionmaking in Planning, Response, and Recovery Activities

The resilience of a community rests on its ability to draw upon its own internal resources in the face of health incidents while also being able to rapidly restore a state of self-sufficiency following a crisis. Given these attributes, participatory citizen engagement in decisionmaking for planning, response, and recovery activities is specifically identified as a key theme within the National Health Security Strategy. Citizen engagement entails the active participation of community residents in response and recovery planning, to ensure that plans reflect the views and perspectives of a wide range of public health system stakeholders, particularly those representing populations who are at risk because of functional limitations (Lyn & Martin, 1991). Communities are more resilient against health threats when all individuals, including those at risk, are involved in planning and empowered to help take responsibility for the health of their family and community.

In addition, community members should be engaged in planning exercises for health incidents, and local social networks should be effectively used to disseminate risk information and aid community members in the response and recovery phases of a health incident. The value of social networks, including the ways in which social media are used to engage and strengthen networks, is also a hallmark of social connectedness and cohesion. Engagement is critical to ensuring accurate, timely, and resilient situational awareness, and should also extend beyond the local level to include multilateral and multinational coordination among stakeholders. Ensuring a broad base of engagement among community members and local organizations supports greater situational awareness and coordination during the response and recovery phases of a disaster.

Another important aspect of citizen engagement is the extent of social connectedness within a community, which refers to the personal (e.g., friend, family, neighbor) and professional (e.g., service provider, community leader) relationships among community residents. Relationships can involve individuals who are similar in status (i.e., horizontal) or individuals of varying status and power (i.e., vertical) (Chandra et al., 2010). The interconnectivity of individuals and organizations contributes to the resilience of a community. For instance, people connected to community organizations and other providers of knowledge and resources perceive themselves to be at higher risk and are therefore more likely to engage in preparedness activities before a disaster (Yong-Chan & Jinae, 2010). In addition, social connectedness increases individuals' access to real and perceived social support, and communities with many social connections can more quickly mobilize needed resources (Putnam, 2000; Magsino, 2009). Community residents and organizations can use personal and professional relationships to send and receive information and to provide instrumental and emotional support during all phases of a disaster. Overall, being part of a healthy community (i.e., one with strong social networks and a sense of community) can improve survival chances and safety of community residents during a disaster (Buckland & Rahman, 1999; Schellong, 2007).

Key elements of community engagement are shown in Table 6.1.

## Activities Related to Community Engagement

Suggested activities relating to each of these elements are discussed in detail below.

### Element 1: Activities to Involve Community Members in Planning and Decisionmaking on Issues Relating to Response and Recovery

This element includes activities that will actively engage community members in how emergency plans are developed and implemented.

**Engage residents in the development of preparedness plans at the individual and community level.**

*Rationale:* Developing plans for health security in the areas of response and recovery requires plans to effectively incorporate input and reflect the views of local community members. This facilitates their likelihood of integration within the daily practice of individuals and organizations.

*Key leaders:* Local government and NGOs.

**Table 6.1**
**Key Elements of Community Engagement**

| Element | Description | Activities for State and Local Entities |
|---|---|---|
| 1. Involve community members in planning and decisionmaking on issues relating to response and recovery activities. | Local government and community organizations actively work to elicit input from local residents and include their feedback in development of plans. Actions or decisions taken reflect an appropriate level of consensus among the local population. | Engage residents in the development of preparedness plans at the individual and community level. Identify geographic concentrations of at-risk individuals. Build the capacity of social and volunteer organizations (i.e., NGOs) to engage citizens in collective action to address an issue or problem (e.g., a community development or service project). |
| 2. Include community members in planning exercises for health incidents. | Residents of the community are encouraged to participate in appropriate exercises and are familiar with planned response and recovery activities. | Involve local community residents in response planning. Develop community exercises that focus on the needs of vulnerable populations. |
| 3. Build connections among social networks and community organizations. | Response and recovery activities have a broader reach when social networks are utilized to promote greater sharing of information and resources. Connections among community organizations and local residents should be reinforced and utilized to quickly disseminate information and offer assistance to those who need it. | Encourage support from local sources for neighbors, friends, and family during nonemergent times. Develop a plan for establishing social routines and relationships in the community after disaster. |

*Potential steps:* Local planners should establish working committees with a representative, cross-sector population to promote more coordinated emergency planning.

**Identify geographic concentrations of at-risk individuals.**

*Rationale:* Incorporating at-risk individuals into planning efforts requires understanding of where these persons are located in the community.

*Key leaders:* State and local government.

*Potential steps:* Identifying geographic concentrations of at-risk individuals with functional needs allows planners to develop effective plans to address their needs and aids in the development and translation of research on critical preparedness and response interventions for all at-risk individuals.

**Build the capacity of social and volunteer organizations (i.e., NGOs) to engage citizens in collective action to address an issue or problem (e.g., a community development or service project).**

*Rationale:* Community experience in successfully confronting challenges within a normal context (day-to-day interactions where residents collectively confront and resolve problems) can help prepare a community to effectively deal with significant changes post-disaster and generate a collective feeling of efficacy among community members.

*Key leaders:* State and local government, and local NGOs.

*Potential steps:* State and local governments should engage in partnerships with NGOs to leverage resources for funding collaboratives, giving attention to opportunities for dual-use purposes in funding health security activities. Increased collaboration and partnerships among local organizations that pursue larger public health goals in addition to preparedness confer the added benefit of stronger coalitions that perform more effectively during disaster response.

**Develop guidance on best practices in active involvement of government and NGOs, including the private sector, in local emergency planning committees or other relevant bodies with a role in health security.**

*Rationale:* Community needs vary widely across regions, and many communities lack a clear vision of optimal strategies to enhance the community's overall resilience by greater organizational involvement, and to prevent, protect from, respond to, and recover from health incidents.

*Key leaders:* Federal and state government, national NGOs.

*Potential steps:* Federal and state governments should issue guidance on expectations for stakeholder involvement, with information on how to assess effective partnerships and how to maximize the roles and benefits of government and nongovernmental leaders on these planning groups or committees. Guidance might also include specific examples from exemplary communities that could be adapted; guidance should provide enough flexibility for local adoption (e.g., identifying existing resources provided by federal, state, and local authorities; determining ways to leverage dollars for dual-use or benefit; building the capacity of NGOs as partners in health security; maximizing resources across government and NGO partnerships).

### Element 2: Activities to Include Community Members in Planning Exercises for Health Incidents

This element focuses on the active engagement of community members in testing and improving community plans.

**Involve local community residents in response planning.**

*Rationale:* Knowing who interacts with whom can be critical for promoting situational awareness and developing coordinated emergency response plans before a disaster occurs. For this to happen, emergency planners need to involve local community members in response planning to determine what social networks exist and how to activate them during a disaster.

*Key leaders:* Local government and NGOs.

*Potential steps:* Planners should also be aware of existing social routines in the community and prioritize efforts to reinforce and restore these routines; such efforts have been shown to increase community resilience. For example, planners should think in family terms, rather than individual terms, and plan accordingly so that shelters, evaluation plans, and even public assistance can be organized around keeping families together, rather than inadvertently splitting them apart.

**Develop community exercises that focus on the needs of vulnerable populations.**

*Rationale:* A critical method for preparing communities is to exercise drills that identify and account for the specific needs of at-risk populations during an emergency, and that include at-risk individuals. Involving at-risk individuals in exercises also can increase trust and cooperation during an actual emergency. Faith-based organizations and other NGOs are examples of community entities with strong ties to the local community that may not have been a part of disaster teams (Baezconde-Garbanati et al., 2006; Pant et al., 2008).

*Key leaders*: Local government and NGOs.

*Potential steps:* Involving at-risk individuals in the planning process improves the efficacy of plans designed to meet the needs of this population, since they bring to the planning process

- knowledge and insights about their needs
- insights into common concerns of individuals with special needs
- advice regarding the appropriate content and format of preparedness materials, risk-communication messages, and alerts
- awareness of equipment and supplies needed by responders and shelter providers (Ringel et al., 2009).

Involving at-risk populations in planning can also decrease the negative psychological impact of disasters by fostering a sense of coping self-efficacy—one's sense of being able to manage the demands of posttraumatic recovery (Benight & Harper, 2002). When plans are made without respect for these concerns, however, the community may spend additional resources that further delay its ability to rebound quickly and effectively.

### Element 3: Activities to Build Connections Among Social Networks and Community Organizations

This element entails activities that are critical to building social connection before and after a disaster. This is a cornerstone of resilience because these connections ensure that communities can restore routine or daily functioning. Many of these activities should be led by local non-governmental organizations.

**Encourage support from local sources for neighbors, friends, and family during nonemergent times.**

*Rationale:* Communities with many social connections can quickly mobilize needed resources for disaster response through local residents (Magsino, 2009). In addition, research has indicated that the decentralized and flexible structure of these local social networks allowed them to respond quickly—and that a centralized, rigid emergency response takes longer to mobilize and can delay the distribution of needed resources, ultimately reducing community resiliency (Baker & Refsgaard, 2007).

*Key leaders:* Local NGOs.

*Potential steps:* Local community organizations should facilitate this resource-sharing and reinforce social networks that can provide crucial community assets during disasters while serving as key sources of emotional support to enhance recovery. Individuals should become educated about their civic responsibility and ask for/offer support as needed.

**Develop a plan for establishing social routines and relationships in the community after disaster.**

*Rationale:* A resilient community can be characterized by its interconnectivity—that is, the presence of strong horizontal and vertical relationships that exist between community residents (Allenby & Fink, 2005). There is evidence that both the sense of community created by these relationships and the individual characteristics of the relationships (i.e., the characteristics of those involved) help improve disaster preparedness (Kim & Kang, 2010).

*Key leaders:* Local NGOs with local government.

*Potential steps:* To promote horizontal social relationships, individuals can get to know their neighbors, and local NGOs can host social events that allow residents to interact. Neighborhood Watch groups, block associations, and other local citizen-led efforts provide opportunities to develop social relationships close to the places that residents frequent (e.g., homes, schools, workplaces) and, along with advocacy groups, can connect residents with decisionmakers (i.e., vertical relationships). Residents could also consider joining a local volunteer group focused on disaster response and recovery, such as a Community Emergency Response Team. To ensure that these social networks are restored quickly after a disaster, recovery efforts should prioritize repairing or rebuilding social and community organizations. To support this prioritization, key social and community organizations should be identified by local emergency planning committees and specifically referenced in response and recovery plans.

# CHAPTER SEVEN

# Self-Sufficiency: Enable and Support Individuals and Communities to Assume Responsibility for Their Preparedness

Self-sufficiency is a critical component of community resilience and entails increasing the capacity of individuals, communities, or institutions to become more self-reliant. In the context of community resilience, the concept of "self" in self-reliance or self-sufficiency can be extended beyond the individual citizen to include the community. The "self" can apply to the individual who stockpiles supplies, the household that develops a household emergency plan, or the community that expects to manage an emergency without immediate external assistance following an incident. To work toward self-sufficiency, individuals should take responsibility for personal preparedness and support the preparedness efforts of other community members. Furthermore, community members and leaders should have reasonable expectations of external support in an incident. Finally, the community should foster a sense of civic responsibility in preparedness and response.

Since September 11, 2001, preparedness communications and guidance have heavily emphasized the need for individuals to play a proactive role in preparedness and response. For example, governmental and nongovernmental information sources across the spectrum, from Ready.gov to Red Cross and AARP, suggest that the general population, as well as at-risk individuals, stockpile supplies and medications, prepare disaster kits, plan for evacuations, and receive first aid training (McGee et al., 2009; FEMA, 2011). The active engagement of individual citizens in response is critical for a variety of reasons. First, individuals on the scene are the true "first responders" to an incident, and communities that are capable of mobilizing a bystander response can mitigate many negative public health impacts (Subcommittee on Economic Development, 2009; Jacob et al., 2008; AufderHeide, 2004; Hesloot & Ruitenberg, 2004). According to FEMA, "Every citizen in this country is part of a national emergency management system" (FEMA, 2004). Second, disaster conditions can prevent the deployment of external aid until the acute phase of the emergency has passed; thus, communities have to improvise response at the local level and leverage existing resources. Finally, communities with a strong sense of civic responsibility and community identity are likely to be cohesive communities with strong social ties, a clear public health ethic (i.e., willingness to make certain individual sacrifices for the greater good), and a firm commitment to place. Cohesion is protective in an incident and encourages communities to make greater investments in recovery.

Traditionally, at-risk individuals are less empowered and more vulnerable to increased harm during a health incident because they are unable to take advantage of disaster preparedness planning, response, and recovery activities normally afforded (Wingate et al., 2007). As Norris and colleagues (2008) indicated, the people who are hardest hit by disasters are those who already find it difficult to meet their family's needs. At-risk individuals should not be expected to assume responsibility for their safety in isolation in the face of disaster; rather, they should be encouraged to take responsibility for their preparedness by accessing their social networks and community resources.

Key elements of self-sufficiency are shown in Table 7.1.

## Activities Related to Self-Sufficiency

Suggested activities relating to each of these elements are discussed in detail below.

### Element 1: Activities to Encourage Personal and Community Preparedness

This element includes four possible activities: (1) develop individual/family plans that identify where reunification will take place; (2) disseminate preparedness materials to community members; (3) incentivize individual preparedness; and (4) conduct and/or sponsor research on appropriate use of Medkits.

**Develop individual/family plans that identify where reunification will take place.**

**Table 7.1**
**Key Elements of Self-Sufficiency**

| Element | Description | Activities for State and Local Entities |
|---|---|---|
| 1. Encourage personal and community preparedness. | Promote and support actions taken by individuals, households, and communities to gain knowledge about potential hazards, prevent adverse consequences, and implement appropriate incident response. | Develop individual/family plans that identify where reunification will take place. Become educated on emergency preparedness and disseminate educational materials received from trainings to community members and neighborhood associations. Incentivize individual and community preparedness. |
| 2. Encourage civic responsibility. | Support actions and attitudes associated with democratic governance and social participation. In the context of national health security, civic responsibility includes actions such as participation in emergency planning and advocacy. | Develop and disseminate messages that foster a sense of civic responsibility in responding to a disaster (e.g., public benefits of vaccination). Emphasize positive messaging as opposed to the negative consequences of inaction. |
| 3. Promote effective bystander responses. | Encourage productive actions to be taken by individuals to protect themselves and other community members during an incident. Bystander response requires that, until emergency responders arrive, communities are sufficiently healthy to sustain themselves and attend to their own health needs (including the need for psychological support), and can assist in addressing the needs of at-risk individuals. | Develop and promote programs that recognize the vital role citizens can and must play as "first responders" to help their own families and neighbors in the first hours to days of a major disaster. |
| 4. Foster self- and community-reliance. | Encourage individuals and communities to assume responsibility for their health and well-being and the health and well-being of their neighbors, and communicate that they should expect to function without external assistance for up to 72 hours after an incident. | Ask for and provide informational, instrumental, and emotional support to/from neighbors, friends, and family. Emphasize a community "call to action" in which individual responsibility is stressed. |

*Rationale:* The quick and efficient reunification of families after a disaster helps to reduce negative mental health outcomes and allows individuals to exert control over their situation (Moore et al., 2004). At the community level, effective response plans promote collective efficacy and help render the situation more comprehensible and manageable.

*Key leaders:* State and local government, local NGOs, and community members.

*Potential steps:* Local organizations and community members should encourage families to develop response plans to designate locations and any action steps for reuniting after a disaster. Similarly, communities should develop a community-level response plan to promote a greater sense of coherence and connectedness in cases of disaster, as well as to promote communication and information sharing.

**Become educated on emergency preparedness and disseminate educational materials received from trainings to community members and neighborhood associations.**

*Rationale:* Educated citizens are aware of critical pre-incident public health messages and where to seek information during an incident. They are also aware of evacuation routes in their community and are trained in basic first aid. Since individuals make up the community, individual preparedness relieves some burden on already taxed response systems, freeing up the responders to dedicate resources in the early stages of an incident to the most vulnerable populations.

*Key leaders:* State and local government, local NGOs, and community members.

*Potential steps:* Individuals and other stakeholders should pursue strategies that incentivize individual efforts to become educated and prepared and help motivate and inform others within the community such as neighbors, family members, and members of social, cultural, and religious groups.

**Incentivize individual and community preparedness.**

*Rationale:* Research suggests that the appropriate, targeted use of incentives can encourage and sustain behavior change (Sutherland, Christianson, & Leatherman, 2008).

*Key leaders:* Federal government, state and local government, NGOs, and researchers.

*Potential steps:* To encourage actions by individuals and communities regarding personal and community preparedness, governments, NGOs, and research institutions should work together to determine and evaluate what incentive structure (e.g., monetary, other) could be used to motivate proactive, self-sufficient behaviors (e.g., storing water) and the movement toward community preparedness. Once there is an evidence base to inform this incentive structure, funding can be allocated for community-level interventions.

**Conduct and/or sponsor research on the utility and appropriate composition of Medkits. Disseminate research to local jurisdictions, NGOs, and individuals to inform individual-level preparedness activities, including the stockpiling of supplies.**

*Rationale:* Resilient communities are prepared for temporary disruptions in vital services, such as electricity and water, and for limited availability of critical supplies such as food and medicine. Although official messages often stress the importance of purchasing disaster kits or stockpiling critical supplies, and various organizations have experimented with providing disaster kits to low-income populations, there is little evidence to suggest these activities result in enhanced individual-level preparedness.

*Key leaders:* Federal government.

*Potential steps:* The federal government should support research regarding the appropriate composition of disaster kits/supplies for various types of hazards.

### Element 2: Activities to Encourage Civic Responsibility

This element includes an activity to foster civic engagement and responsibility.

**Develop and disseminate messages that foster a sense of civic responsibility in responding to a disaster (e.g., public benefits of vaccination). Emphasize positive messaging as opposed to the negative consequences of inaction.**

*Rationale:* Framing messages to emphasize the connections between individual and community preparedness helps motivate community members to take preparedness measures.

*Key leaders:* Federal, state, and local governments and NGOs.

*Potential steps:* Governments, in partnership with nongovernmental organizations such as businesses, should develop these positive messages, test them to ensure they resonate with community members and promote the value of individual and civic responsibility for a community's well-being, and then disseminate them broadly to community members in a variety of formats (radio, newspaper, TV, etc.). The federal government can also begin to provide templates for how to emphasize this connection between individual and community preparedness.

### Element 3: Activities to Promote Effective Bystander Responses

**Develop and promote programs that recognize the vital role citizens can and must play as "first responders" to help their own families and neighbors in the first hours to days of a major disaster.**

*Rationale:* A productive bystander response can greatly reduce the impacts of an incident, and citizens who are prepared to make such a response can support the efforts of traditional first responders (Hesloot & Ruitenberg, 2004). Also, having realistic expectations for external support (i.e., help may not arrive for hours to days) will limit certain negative mental health impacts.

*Key leaders:* Federal, state, and local governments and NGOs.

*Potential steps:* Government as well as NGOs should develop, evaluate, and implement programs to support the role of the citizens as first responders (i.e., provide necessary knowledge, skills, and tools).

### Element 4: Activities to Foster Self- and Community Reliance

These activities center on creating a sense of personal and community reliance and responsibility for preparedness.

**Ask for and provide informational, instrumental, and emotional support to/from neighbors, friends, and family.**

*Rationale:* Research has suggested that communities with many social connections can more quickly mobilize needed resources through local residents (Baker & Refsgaard, 2007; Magsino, 2009). Research has suggested the decentralized and flexible structure of these local social networks allowed them to respond quickly—and that a centralized, rigid emergency response takes longer to mobilize and can delay the distribution of needed resources, ultimately reducing community resiliency (Haines, Hurlbert, & Beggs, 1996).

*Key leaders:* Local NGOs and community members.

*Potential steps:* Local community organizations should facilitate this resource sharing and reinforce social networks that can provide crucial community assets during disasters, while serving as key sources of emotional support to enhance recovery. Individuals should become educated about their civic responsibility and ask for/offer support as needed.

**Emphasize a community "call to action" in which individual responsibility is stressed.**

*Rationale:* Mobilizing communities around individual responsibility serves to increase resilience; in addition, community members will build social connections in the process of mobilization.

*Key leaders:* Federal, state, and local governments and NGOs.

*Potential steps:* Governmental and nongovernmental organizations should use social marketing techniques to mobilize and educate community members around individual responsibility and self-reliance—continuing to emphasize, however, that self-reliance can coexist with willingness to follow official guidance and messaging (e.g., to evacuate a given jurisdiction).

# CHAPTER EIGHT

# Partnership: Develop Strong Partnerships Within and Between Government and Other Organizations

Developing the capacity of a community to prevent, withstand, and mitigate the stress of a health incident is a fundamental element of community resilience. Because much of this capacity may currently exist across a loosely associated system of groups, networks, and organizations, the importance of forming robust partnerships within communities and across government and civil society is a central concern for building community resilience. Researchers have argued that building community resilience entails a process of linking a set of networked adaptive capacities, and that organizational linkages help build collective resilience (Norris et al., 2008). By developing effective partnerships across government and local organizations, communities increase both the volume of resources (by pooling them) and the diversity of resources (via greater amount of variation) (Norris et al., 2008). Resources can come in the form of personnel, land resources, or other forms of in-kind assets.

The National Health Security Strategy (HHS, 2009) asserts that achieving national health security requires an "enterprise"' approach, one that harnesses the full range of government and nongovernmental organizations, communities, and individuals and calls for a high level of integration and coordination among a wide range of organizations. Establishing partnerships between governmental and nongovernmental organizations confers a number of benefits that enhance community resilience. For instance, greater integration of organizations can increase trust and knowledge among community members and help maximize participation in emergency preparedness activities, thus contributing to the ability of communities to enhance plans and speed recovery. In addition, involving new partners in public-private partnerships can increase critical infrastructure through memorandums of understanding prior to a disaster and can thus improve the ability of a community to recover from a disaster. Moreover, engaging local groups and organizations in disaster efforts creates a "unified effort" that could be stronger under distress and result in increased community resiliency. Developing such partnerships can also substantially improve disaster planning for at-risk individuals by engaging the organizations that have the greatest sense of their needs. Last, integration of organizations can enhance nondisaster collaboration, which improves community resilience and well-being. Ultimately, promoting more extensive partnership throughout community and governmental organizations ensures that preparation, response, and recovery activities have a wider reach, with stronger ties to the community and increased knowledge and capacity for support services.

Key elements of effective community partnerships are shown in Table 8.1.

**Table 8.1**
**Key Elements of Effective Community Partnerships**

| Element | Description | Activities for State and Local Entities |
|---|---|---|
| 1. Establish pre-event memorandums of understanding that delineate clear roles and responsibilities among partners. | This helps to establish "ownership" of critical tasks among stakeholders and prevents redundancy and confusion among collaborating organizations during the response and recovery phases of a disaster. | Convene working committees composed of members from the public and private sectors. Identify outcomes and measures of community resilience, as well as local vulnerabilities. |
| 2. When possible, partnership agreements should be supported by a dedicated workforce to implement agreed-upon activities. | Generally, organizations must work to ensure that partnerships are sustainable over time and result in the development of ongoing working relationships. | Identify strategies to build the capacity of NGOs as partners in health security. |
| 3. Assess the extent of existing networks and social routines among community members and organizations, with attention to identifying strategies to reinforce them. | Organizations should also explore effective ways of activating social networks during a disaster. | Determine what social networks exist and how to activate them during a disaster. Conduct vulnerability assessments prior to health incidents. |

## Activities Related to Effective Community Partnerships

Suggested activities relating to each of these elements are discussed in detail below.

### Element 1: Activities to Establish Pre-Event Memorandums of Understanding That Delineate Clear Roles and Responsibilities Among Partners

These activities are designed to promote formalized agreements among potential partners in advance of a health incident, and entail outreach and collaboration between government and nongovernmental organizations to designate effective pre-incident partnerships.

**Build regional healthcare coalitions to ensure that health systems have adequate capacity during response and recovery.**

*Rationale:* The strength of the existing public health system will determine its ability to meet heightened demand during a large health-related incident. Building regional healthcare coalitions can strengthen coordination and communication among multiple stakeholders across regions. Stronger coalitions also help harness a greater pool of human and technical resources that can serve as vital assets during the response phase of a disaster.

*Key leaders:* Federal and state governments.

*Potential steps:* Officials at federal and state levels can convene strong working committees composed of members from the public and private sectors, providing opportunities for networking, information sharing, and pre-event coordination.

**Engage established and local organizations (e.g., cultural, civic, and faith-based groups; schools; and businesses) and social networks to develop and disseminate preparedness information and supplies (e.g., response kits with food provisions).**

*Rationale:* Integrating local organizations that have not been part of disaster planning in the past can engage new partners into health security and increase capacity. In addition, faith-based organizations and other NGOs can have strong knowledge and ties to the local community.

*Key leaders:* State and local governments.

*Potential steps:* Approach local nongovernmental organizations, such as those that traditionally work with at-risk individuals, working with them to improve planning and response efforts for addressing their needs. Leaders should seek to identify trusted sources of information, and encourage public involvement and open communication among all residents during and after a crisis. Moreover, local organizations can be engaged to help train community-based messengers in risk communication principles and engage them to deliver health messages during and after a crisis.

**Establish partnerships between colleges/universities and employers to offer health security–related courses and learning opportunities for practitioners and volunteers to further their education.**

*Rationale:* Health systems rely on the knowledge and skills of the workforce. Workers in health security must receive strong initial training as well as further skill-building opportunities.

*Key leaders:* Federal and state governments.

*Potential steps:* Promote partnerships with institutions of higher education that are designed to develop a broad training framework that articulates professional roles and competencies for health security and offers training and career development paths that will help ensure that current and future workers are prepared to meet the challenges ahead.

**Involve private hospitals, laboratories, and other industries in national, state, territorial, tribal, and local planning efforts to develop integrated situational awareness systems, encouraging use of these systems as they become available.**

*Rationale:* A fundamental challenge to addressing health incidents is the number and diversity of individuals, agencies, and organizations engaged in both routine and incident-related situational awareness. Each stakeholder possesses a different combination of skills, terminology, goals, understanding of responsibilities, and expectations.

*Key leaders:* Federal and state governments.

*Potential steps:* Officials should engage a broad array of healthcare institutions in order to foster effective coordination across sectors, and should promote a collaborative environment for sharing situational awareness information through consideration of funding mechanisms, memorandums of understanding, and addressing the business case for hospital/clinical participation in situational-awareness systems. Effective coordination should build upon a set of common or core guidance and tools, established nationally with appropriate room for local flexibility. These integrated systems would make use of near-real-time information about the characteristics of the evolving health incident itself and the available resources available to respond to the incident.

**Enhance coordination regarding roles and responsibilities and strengthen relationships across levels of government and with NGOs.**

*Rationale:* During and after an incident, the skills and assets of both public and private sectors can benefit the general public and increase resiliency throughout critical supply chains in the community.

*Key leaders:* Federal, state, and local governments.

*Potential steps:* Leaders should seek to coordinate with state, tribal, territorial, and local entities to improve communication, set funding priorities, and identify lead agencies for activities relating to preparedness, response, and recovery. All levels of government should work together in partnership with employers, faith-based organizations, and NGOs to augment the availability of critical services and facilities during disasters, using preexisting social networks and modern social media as tools to augment these linkages. Partnerships can be used to identify outcomes and measures of community resilience as well as local vulnerabilities. Public-private partnerships to increase critical infrastructure can also be developed through memorandums of understanding or contracts of agreement constructed prior to a disaster.

**Involve state and local public health officials in planning at the regional level.**

*Rationale:* Local governments have primary responsibility for disaster response and recovery in their communities and often serve as sources of innovation and best practices in improving preparedness at the community level.

*Key leaders:* The federal government.

*Potential steps:* Guidance from the federal level may delineate the desired level of preparedness for state and local governments and ensure that state and local planners are equipped to manage response and recovery efforts. All levels of government can work to strengthen emergency preparedness and improve emergency response coordination between public health, law enforcement, corrections, and the judiciary.

**Continue coordination of systems and programs to improve and enhance capabilities for repatriation of patients to their original communities following large-scale medical evacuation.**

*Rationale:* Evacuations due to health threats can create large disruptions in local communities, especially for medically vulnerable populations. After the acute stages of disaster, local governments struggle to assist patients and family members in returning to their original communities or care facilities.

*Key leaders:* The federal government.

*Potential steps:* Officials could coordinate with state and local governments to strengthen programs to repatriate medically vulnerable individuals and ensure continuity of care in the transition from response to recovery.

### Element 2: Activities to Support Partnership Agreements with a Dedicated Workforce to Implement Agreed-Upon Activities

The activities below entail efforts that would augment the amount of personnel available to support health security at the state and local levels; they aim to ensure that the health security workforce is culturally competent to address the needs of local communities.

**Partner with institutions serving culturally diverse populations to recruit a diverse workforce into health security–related fields.**

*Rationale:* Understanding and respect for the diversity within communities and the underlying factors that influence hearth are critical to the performance of health security capabilities.

*Key leaders:* Federal, state, and local governments.

*Potential steps:* All stakeholders should focus on ensuring that the national health security workforce is linguistically, culturally, developmentally (e.g., serving children), and economically sensitive to the communities it serves.

**Develop guidance on best practices on the health security workforce, which includes the active involvement of government and NGOs.**

*Rationale:* Local communities can benefit from guidance on engaging stakeholders in effective partnerships.

*Key leaders:* The federal government.

*Potential steps:* Officials can work in partnership with local communities to develop guidance on expectations for stakeholder involvement, with information on how to assess effective partnerships and how to maximize the roles and benefits of government and nongovernmental leaders on these planning groups or committees. Such practices may include financial incentives (e.g., challenge grants) provided by federal, state, and local authorities to build the capacity of NGOs as partners in health security, or incentives to attract businesses to more resilient communities.

### Element 3: Activities to Assess the Extent of Existing Networks and Social Routines Among Community Members and Organizations

The activities within this element entail state and local officials engaging in efforts to examine the networks and supporting social structures currently in place within their communities, which will facilitate greater coordination and improved ability to leverage these resources in the case of an event.

**Assess the location and robustness of social networks, with attention to which community organizations will serve as lead agencies in disseminating risk information and resources to constituents for response and recovery. Designate a user-friendly methodology for assessment that can be used by diverse communities.**

*Rationale:* Knowing who interacts with whom can be critical for promoting situational awareness and developing coordinated emergency response plans before a disaster occurs.

*Key leaders:* State and local governments, and nongovernmental organizations.

*Potential steps:* Emergency planners can involve local community members in response planning to determine what social networks exist and how to activate them during a disaster. Local organizations should take steps to identify existing social routines in the communities they serve and prioritize efforts to reinforce and restore these routines.

**Local government entities should partner with NGOs and private organizations to conduct pre-event vulnerability assessments.**

*Rationale:* Conducting pre-event vulnerability assessments in partnership with local community-based organizations can be particularly useful as local government may have insufficient resources and staff to do so alone.

*Key leaders:* Local governments and nongovernmental organizations.

*Potential steps:* Develop partnerships to conduct vulnerability assessments prior to health incidents. Formal or informal partnerships involving businesses can identify important supply chains to support critical infrastructure and preservation of key resources during an incident.

**Establish a consortium of state, territorial, tribal, and local health departments to compile, implement, and evaluate a suite of low-cost, easy-to-implement innovative practices that allow public health authorities to collect and analyze data relevant to national health security.**

*Rationale:* Near-real-time awareness of a health incident and available resources, in turn, rely on low- and high-technology systems for sharing situational awareness information; these systems must be interoperable, redundant, and reliable.

*Key leaders:* The federal government.

*Potential steps:* Leaders can work to ensure coordination at both the conceptual and technological levels, while ensuring participation and buy-in from a broad range of stakeholders. Federal guidance may establish minimum expectations, keeping in mind the burden that might be imposed on various stakeholders from a resource standpoint. Practices may be grouped into modules, potentially including health status of the community, inventory and readiness status of local response assets, detection of potential and emerging incidents, threat-specific surge in active surveillance, and peri- and post-event situation reports.

# CHAPTER NINE

# Quality: Collect, Analyze, and Utilize Data to Monitor and Evaluate Progress on Building Community Resilience

This chapter offers suggestions for how federal, state, and local organizations that are implementing the community resilience–building activities described in Chapters Three through Eight can monitor and evaluate progress. A community's ability to collect, analyze, and utilize data is a critical lever needed to monitor and evaluate progress on building community resilience. If a community cannot adequately monitor disease incidence and the quality and continuity of care over the course of response, then its ability to recover quickly is compromised (Williams, 2008). Understanding of the pre- and post-disaster physical health state of the community (e.g., the percentage of community members with chronic conditions requiring home care) can inform preparedness plans as well as expectations for the length of a specific community's recovery period (Chandra & Acosta, 2009).

Over time, monitoring and evaluation of community health can help to build the evidence base for and improve community resilience (Brownson, Fielding, & Maylahn, 2009). In previous chapters, we have described numerous gaps in the evidence base associated with community resilience (e.g., limited empirical evidence about the critical subcomponents of resilience). More research and evaluation can help to answer key questions (e.g., what are the most cost-effective and impactful ways to build community resilience) and will inform communities' decisionmaking and resource allocation. Monitoring of staff performance and competency is important to build resilience in the public health system, which depends upon the ability of people to successfully employ the operational capabilities and accomplish the key activities that support resilience (Chandra et al., 2010).

As the evidence base is developed, these data can be used for continuous quality improvement (CQI) to improve plans and provide lessons that can be applied to improve future efforts. For example, data on population vulnerabilities can help improve mitigation strategies before a disaster (Lindsay, 2003). Social network data could be used to determine which networks are in place, which need to be built, and how these can be used for communications during and after an incident. Tracking a set of relationship indicators (e.g., membership, network interaction, role of the health department, strategic value of partners, trust, reciprocity) over time will provide communities with information that can be used to evaluate current networks and provide guidance to support adjustments to improve collaborative partnerships (Varda et al., 2008).

A strong quality improvement system will require some effort at the federal level for design, data collection, and aggregation of lessons learned for use by communities. Therefore this chapter outlines activities for both federal and local entities.

Key elements of quality are shown in Table 9.1.

**Table 9.1**
**Key Elements of Monitoring and Evaluating Progress in Building Community Resilience**

| Element | Description | Activities for State and Local Entities |
| --- | --- | --- |
| 1. Monitor continuity/quality of care and long-term health effects before, during, and after a health incident. | This includes the regular monitoring of health indicators and health services. | Integrate core data elements relating to health, behavioral health, and social recovery into disaster plans. Partner with universities to identify local sources of data that could inform response and recovery planning and integrate them into a single database. |
| 2. Regularly conduct research and evaluation to advance science and practice associated with community resilience. | Research and evaluation should address gaps in the evidence base, inform decisionmaking and resource allocation, and help determine staff performance and competency. | Regularly collect community resilience measures to determine baseline levels of community resilience and any improvement that occurs. |
| 3. Use monitoring, research, and evaluation data for CQI. | Data can be used to inform plans, expectations for the length of a specific community's recovery period, and future response and recovery. | Share resilience and recovery-related lessons within and across communities. Utilize CQI programs, tools, and techniques to improve community resilience–building activities. |

## Activities Related to Quality

Suggested activities relating to each of these elements are discussed in detail below.

### Element 1: Activities to Monitor Continuity/Quality of Care and Long-Term Health Effects After a Health Incident

These activities pertain to health quality before, during, and after a health security incident.

**Ensure that all disaster plans have identified common data elements (e.g., benchmarks for disaster operations, relevant data from response) to facilitate seamless monitoring and evaluation of health, behavioral health, and social services before, during, and after an incident, and begin developing tools to support state and local recovery planning groups' integration of these elements into their disaster plans.**

*Rationale:* Seamless monitoring and evaluation of health, behavioral health, and social services is critical to ensure that individuals receiving services have continuity of care and that disjointed care does not disrupt healing. Providing disjointed or disconnected services before, during, and after an incident can incur additional costs and compound negative impacts on quality of life.

*Key leaders:* Federal government, and state and local public health departments.

*Potential steps:* Federal, state, and local decisionmakers should define the common core elements of health, behavioral health, and social recovery as well as the key data elements that should be included in all community disaster plans. Tools are needed to help state and local recovery groups integrate these indicators into their disaster plans.

**Build the capacity of local communities to better utilize existing data on health, behavioral health, and social services from FEMA and other state and local sources.**

*Rationale:* Up-to-date information is critical to communities that are planning for adequate physical and psychological healthcare to help mitigate impacts of disaster. Plans should be developed based on an understanding of the current health and health needs of the population, the location of vulnerable populations, and potential psychological risks (e.g., social isolation).

*Key leaders:* Federal government and local health departments.

*Potential steps:* At the federal level, HHS and federal partners should review federal databases to identify additional data that need to be linked to the National Emergency Management Information System (NEMIS). Plans need to be developed to link shared data concerning recovery assessments, services provided during the response (e.g., to NEMIS), and recovery outcomes (e.g., the data linked with recovery plans). At the local level, the health department should partner with universities to identify local sources of data that could inform response and recovery planning and integrate them into a single database.

### Element 2: Activities to Conduct Research and Evaluation

Activities to address this element include enhancing efforts concerning research and evaluation.

**Convene representatives from national and local NGOs along with cross-sector federal entities to identify key outcomes for and measures of community resilience.**

*Rationale:* Community resilience is an outcome of community engagement and should be embraced across the federal government. Integrating the ideas of representatives from various national and local NGOs and cross-sector federal entities can lead to better planning around the relatively unknown area of community resilience.

*Key leaders:* Federal government, national, and local nongovernmental organizations.

*Potential steps:* To facilitate this process, the federal government across all agencies should hire professional staff to encourage, support, and inform resilience-building activities. The federal government should convene representatives in focus groups, webinars, and other stakeholder formats to elicit ideas and identify key outcomes to measure resilience.

**Pilot test proposed community resilience metrics.**

*Rationale:* There are currently no validated metrics of community resilience. Establishing a set of core metrics for community resilience is a necessary next step to inform systematic evaluation of community resilience–building activities and research studies on community resilience.

*Key leaders:* Federal and local government.

*Potential steps:* Included in this document in Chapter Eleven are proposed measures of community resilience. The local government, with guidance from federal government, should regularly collect these measures (or a subset of these measures) to determine baseline levels of community resilience and any improvement that occur. These measures can also be used to develop future research studies about community resilience. Potential directions for future research are discussed in Chapter Twelve.

### Element 3: Activities to Use Monitoring, Research, and Evaluation Data for Continuous Quality Improvement

These activities principally focus on developing a system for ongoing monitoring and evaluation of community resilience–building activities.

**Develop a centralized and accessible system to aggregate the resilience- and recovery-related lessons learned from local communities (e.g., after-action reports) and disseminate these lessons to communities with accompanying tools/supports and incentives to use them.**

*Rationale:* A key component of resilience is the ability to incorporate lessons learned back into practice as part of a CQI framework (Chandra et al., 2010). Establishing a national system (e.g., a web-based portal) that not only aggregates these lessons at a community level but also allows communities to share lessons learned is integral to continuous improvement of the quality of resilience-building activities. The llis.gov system is used by many communities, but stakeholders shared that it is not organized to provide the concrete or operational information they may need for resilience-building specifically. Many communities are already implementing community resilience–building activities and learning about what works. Having an accessible system is particularly important because the evidence base for community resilience is evolving, so there are few "best practices" currently available (Cutter et al., 2008). This system will contribute to the identification of these best practices.

*Key leaders:* Federal government.

*Potential next steps:* The federal government should partner with national, state, and local nongovernmental organizations to develop and pilot a system to capture lessons learned. This could include a web-based component, and the accompanying tools/supports could utilize the social networking software (e.g., Facebook) that allows groups to share real-time information in a virtual environment.

**Review existing CQI programs and tools/techniques and, if needed, identify and support development of new tools.**

*Rationale*: Quality improvement programs and tools/techniques can help to maximize communities' learning from past events by ensuring that lessons learned are continuously applied to future efforts. Being able to incorporate lessons learned and continuously improve on activities that are being implemented is critical in a nascent field like community resilience where effective strategies and activities are still in the process of being tested and validated.

*Key leaders*: Federal government (HHS and partners).

*Potential next steps*: HHS and federal partners should conduct a review to identify existing tools that incorporate CQI and have demonstrated success. These tools will then be distributed to local communities to apply to their community resilience–building activities.

**Disseminate and incorporate CQI training and tools into community resilience grant guidance and education/training programs.**

*Rationale:* Communities need appropriate supports, such as training and tools, to learn how to fully engage in CQI. Funders and educators can ensure that community leaders have access to these important opportunities by including them in grant guidance and education/training programs.

*Key leaders:* HHS, foundations, and other funders.

*Potential next steps:* Where consistent with relevant statutes and regulations, HHS should encourage all agencies and other entities funding community resilience–building to require grantees to demonstrate the use of CQI processes or tools as a condition of funding. HHS should convene professional associations to identify opportunities to embed CQI principles and tools into their grant and educational programs and to encourage these organizations to develop recognition programs to highlight exemplary CQI practices in community resilience–building.

# CHAPTER TEN

# Efficiency: Leverage Existing Community Resources for Maximum Use and Effectiveness

A focus on community resilience will require not only a new level of engagement from a diverse set of community stakeholders but also an investment—of time, money, and personnel resources—in supporting and bolstering resilience. Monetary and other investments in community resilience must be made efficiently. In a resource-limited environment, such as that facing communities across the nation at the time of this writing, it is necessary to identify activities, partnerships, and resources with dual benefit to improve both health security planning as well as other community health priorities (Baezconde-Garbati et al., 2006; Pant et al., 2008). In addition, an emphasis on efficiency can motivate creativity and partnerships as governmental and nongovernmental organizations collaborate to identify and build on existing resources (Varda et al., 2008). Developing sustainable processes and resilience-strengthening activities requires an integration of any new efforts within the foundation already established by existing organizations. The lever of *efficiency* is an important one to consider when developing a community resilience strategy; in short, determining the best ways to leverage resources is critical across the other levers described in this roadmap. The considerations in this chapter are important for local, state, and federal planners and should serve as an underpinning of all community resilience–building efforts. As denoted in Figure 2.2, both *quality* and *efficiency* are reflected throughout the entire resilience-building process.

Greater efficiency is particularly needed in the processes involved in recovery from a health incident because significant human and financial costs can be incurred as a result of gaps in services or unnecessary redundancies (Chandra & Acosta, 2009). There is also a need for a national framework to leverage resources for recovery. At the time of this writing, there is an effort under way to develop this framework with the White House Disaster Recovery Initiative. This may include preestablished contracts and/or memorandums of understanding for services to transition from response to recovery. Established contracts could encourage a more efficient, timely, and coordinated local response. Communities need to assess which organizations will be reliable for response, although national criteria need to be developed for this assessment. In addition, in light of economic stressors and limited resources, guidance on how to leverage existing assets is needed.

Key elements of efficiency are shown in Table 10.1.

## Activities Related to Efficiency

Suggested activities relating to each of these elements are discussed in detail below.

**Table 10.1**
**Key Elements of Efficiency**

| Element | Description | Activities for State and Local Entities |
|---|---|---|
| 1. Clearly delineate transition and funding processes for response and recovery. | This includes procedures and funding plans for nongovernmental organizations, particularly in terms of how funds are distributed from federal and state government to local entities. | Develop national guidance for transition to recovery planning in the initial phases of any disaster response. Provide funding to NGOs to include health security as part of their effort to improve community resilience and to develop disaster plans. Develop policies for effective donation management. |
| 2. Develop monitoring systems to determine where resources are needed. | This capability will allow communities to marshal resources appropriately to areas of community and not to expend assets unnecessarily. | Develop plans to assess community needs for resource allocation at the onset of an incident to activate funding plans quickly. |

### Element 1: Activities to Support Clear Delineation of Transition and Funding Processes for Response and Recovery

These activities primarily focus on guidance in recovery planning, but similar principles about clarifying organizational roles and responsibilities apply across the preparedness spectrum.

**Develop national guidance for transition to recovery planning in the initial phases of any disaster response.**

*Rationale:* Appropriate planning for long-term recovery of health and social functioning helps to mitigate delays in reconstruction. The planning can also address unmet physical and psychological health needs that may grow into serious issues when left unattended.

*Key leaders:* Federal government with state and local government and nongovernmental partners.

*Potential next steps:* Guidance should outline when and how state and local government and nongovernmental organizations should assume roles and responsibilities for providing citizen services, especially when federal and state government involvement recedes. This includes a coordinated plan for transition to recovery that identifies appropriate resources needed for

- long-term recovery
- priorities for health infrastructure relocation and replacement
- processes to monitor compounding disaster consequences
- recovery strategies that promote long-term social and economic recovery.

In addition to outlining the responsibility hand-off between federal/state and local organizations, this transition to recovery planning should also include processes for engaging local residents in recovery as relief workers and outside contractors leave. Communities also need to work with federal and state governments to develop transition plans to streamline disbursement of funds and transition roles for long-term recovery, particularly to ensure seamless transition between acute incident response periods, longer-term recovery, and return to routine community functioning.

**Provide funding to NGOs to include health security as part of their effort to improve community resilience and to develop disaster plans.**

*Rationale:* Local NGOs connect community members with key services and resources, helping to restore social routines following disasters. NGOs are also able to tailor resilience-building activities to local needs using their regional knowledge and connection with the community. Federal and state funding is needed to help communities build the capacity to participate or lead these efforts, while ensuring that communities determine their own priority activities.

*Key leaders:* Local NGOs, local government with state and federal support.

*Potential next steps:* Although planning before a disaster must be started at the community level, many disasters overwhelm the capabilities of local government. Using a "bottom-up" approach, communities can identify NGOs able to offer additional capacity. State and federal governments should support capacity-building efforts at the local level.

**Develop policies for effective donation management and provide the public with clear guidance on donations (i.e., what the public should donate to the recovery effort and why), particularly to support health and social recovery.**

*Rationale:* In the period following major disasters, heightened public interest often leads to substantial flows of cash and in-kind donations, such as clothing and other equipment, to local and national NGOs involved in response and recovery efforts, . Although most NGO operations rely largely on donations on a day-to-day basis, having clear strategies and guidelines for managing a large influx of donations provides a critical framework for resource allocation during disasters.

*Key leaders:* Federal government and local and national NGOs.

*Potential next steps:* The federal government should work with national and community-level NGOs to develop streamlined systems to identify needed resources for health and social services and to channel donations efficiently to response and recovery activities. In addition, NGOs should communicate clear guidelines to donors and the general public on the most effective and efficient means of donating resources and in-kind support, while ensuring transparency on how such resources are managed. This process could also describe protections against misuse of funds.

**Continue to develop and publish materials that enhance preparedness for emergency response and the transition to health and social service recovery (including alert, activation, deployment, and deactivation/demobilization).**

*Rationale:* Traditional emergency planning has not clearly articulated the time point or "triggers" for transition from response to recovery, the roles and responsibilities during transition, or the operational processes needed to ensure a smooth and efficient transition. Federal guidance (in the form of Assistant Secretary for Preparedness and Response/Office of Preparedness and Emergency Operations playbooks) can help clarify the transition from response to recovery process, including the timing of the "responsibility transition points" among federal, state, and local governments as well as nongovernmental partners. This is particularly critical for health and social service provision, to avoid gaps in services that leave unmet physical and psychological health needs that can develop into serious issues when unattended.

*Key leaders:* Federal government.

*Potential next steps:* The federal government could develop protocols that facilitate this transition by

- identifying appropriate resources needed for long-term human recovery, particularly health and social services, and determine how these resources will be provided to state and local governments
- identifying priorities for health infrastructure relocation and replacement
- developing processes to monitor the compounding consequences of a disaster
- inventorying recovery strategies that promote long-term health and social recovery.

### Element 2: Activities to Develop Monitoring Systems to Determine Where Assets Are Needed

It is also important for communities to strengthen systems that identify and locate assets, not only for effective response but to appropriately deploy resources where they are most needed.

**Develop plans to assess community needs for resource allocation at the onset of an incident to activate funding plans quickly.**

*Rationale:* While it is important to develop plans for transition processes, a key activity to support greater efficiency at the community level is to determine which "hot spots" in a community need resources and when. This ability will allow for quicker response and accelerated recovery.

*Key leaders:* Local government and NGOs.

*Potential next steps:* This activity could begin with the creation of local government and NGO partnerships (or could build on existing partnerships) to identify processes for designating response-reliable agencies that address the needs of the population, including at-risk individuals. In addition, by developing and relying on preestablished contracts or some type of predetermined agreement, federal and state agencies can work with local health, behavioral health, and social service providers to more effectively manage response and recovery.

# CHAPTER ELEVEN

# Future Directions: Implementation, Measurement, and Next Steps

In this chapter, we describe some of the critical questions to consider when developing a local community resilience plan. As communities review this roadmap, it is important to determine an approach to implementation, including monitoring and evaluating implementation and determining the effectiveness of particular activities. The chapter also includes a brief summary of the questions that remain unanswered for the field of community resilience and national health security.

## Implementation of Community Resilience–Building Activities

Once a community plan is developed or modified based on this roadmap, it is essential that communities answer these questions:

1. *How will we know if these activities are working?* There is limited evidence about what works to build community resilience (Chandra et al., 2010). Therefore, the suggested activities proposed here should be monitored to determine their impact on communities. Determining which activities result in productive outcomes can help refine individual community efforts—and efforts nationwide—over time. Although measures of community resilience are currently limited, we provide some potential measures associated with each lever in Table 11.1, which will be discussed below.

2. *What capacities are needed for communities to implement community resilience–building activities?* Communities must implement activities within the existing public health system, which has significant resource and capacity limitations (Salinsky, 2010). Later in this chapter, we describe some issues involving the public health system that might be potential challenges to community resilience–building.

3. *How long will it take communities to achieve full implementation of community resilience–building activities?* Implementing community resilience activities takes time. In order to appropriately gauge expectations, a richer understanding of the process of implementation is needed. In this chapter, we describe a model for implementation that is intended to help policymakers and decisionmakers develop appropriate expectations for the length of time it will take for implementation (Simpson, 2002).

In the remainder of this chapter, we discuss these three questions in more detail.

### How Will We Know If Community Resilience–Building Activities Are Working?

Measurement of community resilience is essential for the operationalization and implementation of community resilience. First, measurement will allow communities, states, and the nation as a whole to assess hypothesized links between inputs into the community resilience process from Figure 2.2 (e.g., community partnerships and education of community members) and outcomes (e.g., greater resilience). Second, measurement is critical to track progress in building community resilience at the local level.

Any proposed measures of community resilience will be developmental. Although this report attempts to outline the inputs into the community resilience process and to define the outputs/outcomes, this framework has not been tested empirically. Most of the literature summarized to describe community resilience—including the definition, attributes, and related activities—is conceptual or theoretically based.

Table 11.1 summarizes some potential areas of measurement for community resilience. Note that this list is intended not to be exhaustive but merely to highlight relevant examples. These areas are organized according to the eight levers of community resilience described in this report, and they include baseline/vulnerability measures as well as measures of health department activities and actions. These measurement areas were derived from the literature review and focus group discussion. While these resources uncovered many candidate measures, Table 11.1 includes only those measures that were clear, had face validity, and for which data could be feasibly collected. Appendix D includes the precise wording of proposed measures, as well as potential data sources.

Testing of these measures will be needed to develop the evidence base, refine the measures, and inform the next generation of measures. Developing a clear understanding of the inputs and outputs in the community resilience–building process will assist in selecting and prioritizing community resilience measures.

### What Capacities Are Needed for Communities to Implement Community Resilience–Building Activities?

Much as in traditional public health practice, implementing community resilience–building activities requires the capacity to build and maintain strong and reliable partnerships (the partnership lever); mobilize community members (the engagement lever); and use data and information for evaluation, monitoring, and decisionmaking (the quality lever).

As discussed in Chapter Six, strong and reliable partnerships involving a diverse array of public, private, governmental, and nongovernmental organizations (e.g., academic institutions, healthcare providers, advocacy groups, media outlets, businesses) are needed to build community resilience. Lessons learned from traditional public health have shown that collaborative models have benefits, but less is known about how roles and responsibilities can best be distributed among the organizations involved in implementing community resilience–building activities. In addition, the strength of collaborative relationships varies widely based on the size of the community and type of partnering organization (Salinsky, 2010). Therefore, in building partnerships, communities will have to consider questions such as the following:

- Who should take the lead in establishing partnerships (e.g., between colleges/universities and employers, regional healthcare coalitions) for a specific community resilience building–activity?
- How should community resilience–building activities vary across and within communities with different characteristics (e.g., size, exposure to disaster)?

**Table 11.1**
**Levers and Proposed Measurement Areas**

| Lever | Proposed Measurement Area |
|---|---|
| Wellness | Disability status |
| | Poverty level |
| | Health status of the population |
| Access | Health insurance coverage |
| | Availability of healthcare providers in medically underserved areas |
| Education | Level of health literacy in the population |
| | Communication vulnerability/non-English-speaking households |
| | Dissemination of risk information and subsequent uptake or use of information |
| Engagement | Identification of at-risk individuals through governmental and nongovernmental engagement |
| | Health department identification of at-risk population "hot spots" |
| | Health department identification of organizations that can serve at-risk population "hot spots" |
| | Social connectedness of general population for disaster response and recovery |
| | Voting behavior |
| Self-Sufficiency | Health department education with at-risk populations |
| | Public's ability to act upon official messages/vulnerability |
| | Level of citizen preparedness and sense of self-reliance |
| Partnership | Local Emergency Planning Committee (LEPC) composition |
| | Role of NGOs in community response and recovery plans |
| Quality | Time to new normalcy (post-incident) |
| | Community's ability to integrate lessons learned from previous incidents |
| Efficiency | Use of public health dollars for dual benefit (public health promotion activities and community resilience–building activities) |

Engagement and self-sufficiency also require the capacity to mobilize partnerships. Models such as Mobilizing for Action through Planning and Partnership (MAPP),[1] a community-wide assessment and strategic planning tool for improving health, have been developed to support community mobilization efforts (Mays, 2010). However, engagement and self-sufficiency require dedicated and sustainable resources, committed leadership, and sophisticated communication skills (Salinsky, 2010). When planning to implement community resilience–building activities, communities should consider which organizations have the time and resources to create and sustain partnerships needed for engagement and self-sufficiency.

Finally, state and local health agencies are increasingly utilizing performance standards, measures, monitoring, and quality improvement processes. A 2005 assessment showed that 55 percent of local health agencies engage in some kind of formal performance assessment (Padgett et al., 2005). However, the most common type of data collected was customer satisfaction surveys. Further capacity-building is needed to ensure that local health agencies can use data to identify internal capacity development needs and monitor the causes of diseases, the magnitude of risk factors, and the relative impact of specific interventions (Salinsky, 2010). All these tasks are critical for moving toward more evidence-based and effective practice and

---

[1] The MAPP process provides communities with a framework for four health assessments that help build their capacity to (1) collect and analyze health data, (2) identify and prioritize community health issues, and (3) develop and implement action plans that address defined needs.

ultimately toward building a more resilient community (Brownson, Fielding, & Maylahn, 2009).

### How Long Will It Take for Communities to Achieve Full Implementation of Community Resilience–Building Activities?

To gauge expectations for community resilience–building efforts, it is helpful to draw guidance from a model of implementation that outlines the stages that a community must pass through before full implementation is achieved (Simpson, 2002). *Full implementation* in this context is meant to describe the evolution of community resilience–building activities starting small with a core group of individuals in a community (e.g., public health department staff) and spreading out to be an activity around which the full community is mobilized (e.g., multiple sectors are involved, including community members). Full implementation will take varying amount of time depending on the baseline levels of mobilization in a community. Determining baseline levels of mobilization in one's community means answering such questions as the following: Do members of my community know what activities are needed to build community resilience? Do they have the capacities needed to implement activities from the other chapters of this document?

When planning a timeline for full implementation, planners can utilize the stages from the Simpson Transfer Model—in which diffusion happens in four stages: exposure, adoption, implementation, and practice (Simpson, 2002)—as possible steps needed for each community resilience–building activity in their plan. First, communities must be exposed to an activity (e.g., through presentation, forum, media). Second, communities will need to build the capacity to adopt activities to build resilience. For example, during this stage a capacity assessment would help determine whether a community has the capacities needed to implement the community resilience–building activities planners have selected. Once organizations have the capacity to implement community resilience–building activities, they begin early implementation. Planners should build in activities that focus on CQI during this stage, which will aid communities still identifying what works best for their community. Finally, communities should consider how to institutionalize the most effective activities. Evaluation is an important part of this stage and can help planners prioritize activities. Movement through such a model takes time, and communities, as well as state and federal organizations, need to take these steps into account. Appropriate monitoring and evaluation, using the measures described above, can help communities assess what stage of implementation they are in and gauge outcomes accordingly.

## Future Research Directions

The existing research has identified ways of strengthening community resilience, including options for strengthening ongoing efforts and planning. But further research is needed to address gaps in existing knowledge. Clarification in these areas, organized around the key levers, should identify best practices in community resilience–building and should measure the overall effect of increasing community resilience. For example, based on identified knowledge gaps in the literature review and stakeholder meetings, the following questions are arranged by lever:

**Wellness and Access:** What are the best ways to frame preparedness in the context of wellness messaging? How should communities convey the connection between individual/family and community preparedness?

**Education:** How do we link better risk communication with improved community resilience?

**Engagement:** How can we use advanced technologies, including new social media, to inform the public, facilitate the social reengagement of people following disasters, and promote social connectedness?

**Self-Sufficiency:** What are the best means to incentivize individual and community preparedness? What policies, including financial and other incentives, will work?

**Partnership:** What is the best way to integrate nongovernmental organizations in planning, and what is the most effective way to assess the capacities and capabilities of specific NGO partners?

**Quality and Efficiency:** What are the best metrics for monitoring and evaluating resilience-building activities? Which baseline data are most critical for assessing key community resilience components and elements?

## Conclusion

This study represents an important step forward in identifying the critical elements of community resilience to support national health security and offers a practical list of potential activities for building resilience before a disaster. Our analysis provides an operational definition upon which progress toward community resilience development can be tracked and a list of strategies intended to bolster the requisite set of capacities and capabilities that communities need to respond to and recover from a health security incident.

The study also suggests several areas in which the evidence base for community resilience needs to be strengthened. Although existing literature provides critical insight into the factors necessary for building community resilience, much of the work is either conceptual or theoretical in nature, and there are far fewer empirical studies. The few studies that assess these topics tend to be retrospective and do not allow for comparative analysis. There is also the challenge of further defining and prioritizing the critical subcomponents of resilience in the context of health security. Analyses are needed to identify and test activities that will help communities strengthen their resilience. Given the ongoing issue of limited resources, crystallizing these priority activities is the next step to moving communities toward this NHSS resilience goal.

The existing research has identified ways of strengthening community resilience, including options for strengthening ongoing efforts and planning. Further research is needed to address gaps in existing knowledge. Clarification in these areas, organized around the key levers, should identify best practices in community resilience–building and should measure the overall effect of increasing community resilience.

# Literature Review and Abstraction

Table A.1 outlines the search strategy used to identify the peer-reviewed and "gray" literature and the relevant regulations and statutes. It also describes the inclusion criteria used in our analysis.

Of the more than 464 citations identified by our search strategy, 144 met criterion A. These citations represented the broad literature on community aspects pertaining to social connectedness, social integration, physical and psychological health, risk communication, mitigation of health risk, and social and economic equity. To identify which of these specifically addressed community resilience or factors of community resilience and disaster preparedness, the review team conducted a second, more thorough, abstract review of these 144 citations. Eighty-six were determined to substantially address community resilience or one of the six components thought to enhance resilience and represented the final literature sample for full review.

The citations that met criteria A and B were reviewed further for information about components thought to enhance community resilience and working definitions of community resilience. Of the 86 citations, 13 contained information about social connectedness, 12 contained information about social integration, 48 contained information about physical or psychological health of the community, 15 contained information about risk communication, 7 contained information about social and economic equity, and 3 contained information about mitigating neighborhood health risk. Sixteen citations contained additional information about

**Table A.1**
**Literature Review and Abstraction**

| | Search and/or Abstraction Criteria | Number of Items |
|---|---|---|
| Initial search | [community OR neighborhood] AND [resilience OR social capital OR collective efficacy OR social cohesion OR connectedness OR community networks OR assets OR strengths-based OR teamwork OR supportive leadership OR measurements OR health literacy OR health competence] AND [preparedness OR emergency OR disaster OR mitigation] | 464 |
| Criterion A | Does the article provide a definition of community resilience? OR Does the article provide information on one of the following factors of community resilience: social connectedness, level of social integration, health of community, effective risk communication, mitigation of health risk, or social and economic equity? | 144 |
| Criterion B | Does the article provide a definition of community resilience or provide empirical or conceptual information that links resilience factors to community preparedness? | 86 |

community resilience that did not pertain specifically to one of the key components of community resilience. Seventeen citations contained a definition of community resilience.

After identifying factors associated with community resilience (see Chandra et al., 2010 for more thorough review of data abstraction processes), we conducted a more narrow review of the literature to identify strategies, tools, and indicators that could be used to measure community resilience. We reviewed more than 30 community resilience–related articles and websites that included a discussion of measurement and then identified and reviewed measurement literature related to the individual core components (e.g., risk communication). All measures referenced in the literature—whether regularly used in a national survey or simply suggested in a conceptual paper—were included in a measures databank that classified each measure by core component.

# Community Resilience Definitions: Findings from Literature Review

The following pages contain capability-based and capacity-based definitions from our literature review.

**Table B.1**
**Capability-Based Definitions**

| Source | Capability Definition | Element 1: Ability to absorb/resist a disaster | Element 2: Ability to maintain basic functions during a disaster | Element 3: Ability to respond | Element 4: Ability to recover, including ability to engage in positive change and move on after disaster | Element 5: Ability to mitigate threats |
|---|---|---|---|---|---|---|
| Berke & Campanella, 2006 | *Achieving resiliency in a disaster context means the ability to survive future natural disasters with minimum loss of life and property, as well as the ability to create a greater sense of place among residents; a stronger, more diverse economy; and a more economically integrated and diverse population.* | | | | | x |
| Bonanno, 2004 | Resilience reflects the ability to *maintain a stable equilibrium.* | x | | | | |
| Community and Regional Resilience Institute, n.d. | *The capability to anticipate risk, limit impact, and bounce back rapidly through survival, adaptability, evolution, and growth in the face of turbulent change.* | x | | x | x | x |
| Community and Regional Resilience, Institute. n.d. | When a community is truly resilient, it should be able to *avoid the cascading system failures to help minimize any disaster's disruption to everyday life and the local economy. A resilient community is not only prepared to help prevent or minimize the loss or damage to life, property and the environment, but also it has the ability to quickly return citizens to work, reopen businesses, and restore other essential services needed for a full and swift economic recovery.* | x | | | x | x |
| Dawes, Cresswell, & Cahan, 2004 | The capacity of a human community, whether a city, a region, or some other collectivity, to *sustain itself through crises that challenge its physical environment and social fabric.* | x | | | | |

**Table B.1—Continued**

| Source | Capability Definition | Element 1: Ability to absorb/resist a disaster | Element 2: Ability to maintain basic functions during a disaster | Element 3 Ability to respond | Element 4: Ability to recover, including ability to engage in positive change and move on after disaster | Element 5: Ability to mitigate threats |
|---|---|---|---|---|---|---|
| Gilbert, 2008 | Resilience is capacity to *find solutions, resist hardship, care, restore function, learn new skills, change, and survive.* | x | | x | x | |
| Keim, 2008 | Vulnerability to natural disasters has two sides: the degree of exposure to dangerous hazards (susceptibility) and the capacity to cope with or recover from the consequences of disasters (resilience). *Disaster resilience is composed of (1) the absorbing capacity, (2) the buffering capacity, and (3) response to the event and recovery from the damage sustained.* | x | | x | x | x |
| Manyena, 2006 | [D]isaster resilience could be viewed as the *intrinsic capacity of a system, community or society predisposed to a shock or stress to adapt and survive by changing its non-essential attributes and rebuilding itself.* | x | | | x | |
| Masten & Obradovic, 2008 | In ecology, resilience [refers to] "the capacity of *a system to absorb disturbance and reorganize and yet persist in a similar state.*" This definition emphasizes persistence or recovery to a similar state. | x | x | | x | |
| National Research Council, 2006 | Resilience can be understood as a response to stress and can be considered as (1) a theory that guides the understanding of stress response dynamics; (2) a set of adaptive capacities that call attention to the resources that promote successful adaptation in the face of adversity; and (3) a strategy for disaster readiness to prepare for unpredictable and difficult to prepare for dangers. | | | x | | |

**Table B.1—Continued**

| Source | Capability Definition | Element 1: Ability to absorb/resist a disaster | Element 2: Ability to maintain basic functions during a disaster | Element 3: Ability to respond | Element 4: Ability to recover, including ability to engage in positive change and move on after disaster | Element 5: Ability to mitigate threats |
|---|---|---|---|---|---|---|
| Pfefferbaum et al., 2008 | Resilience refers to the ability to adapt successfully to adversity, trauma, and threat. It involves attitudes, behaviors, and skills that can be cultivated, taught, and practiced . . . It is not the absence of adversity and distress that characterizes resilience; rather, it is the ability to recover and progress that is its hallmark. Resilience is not an end state but a dynamic process of interdependent forces—at the individual, family, group, and community levels—that continually shape and reshape the organism. *Community resilience [is] the ability of social units to mitigate the effects of hazards and to initiate recovery activities that limit social disruption and the effects of future events.* More than individual coping, community resilience involves interaction as a collective unit . . . consists of both reactive and proactive elements that join recovery from adversity with individual and group efforts to transform their environments to mitigate future problems or events . . . implies a potential to grow from adversity that derives, in part, from deliberate, meaningful cooperation and action. . . . in some situations, failure to change could represent a lack of resilience | | | | x | x |
| Schoch-Spana, 2008 | is refined to mean the *ability to survive and cope with a disaster with minimum impact and damage.* It incorporates the capacity to reduce or avoid losses, contain effects of disasters, and recover with minimal social disruptions.<br><br>Community resilience is the ability of a community to *rebound from a disaster with a new focus on recovery and mitigation and a renewed sense of trust in government* and other community leadership. | | | | x | x |

**Table B.1—Continued**

| Source | Capability Definition | Element 1:<br>Ability to absorb/resist a disaster | Element 2:<br>Ability to maintain basic functions during a disaster | Element 3:<br>Ability to respond | Element 4:<br>Ability to recover, including ability to engage in positive change and move on after disaster | Element 5:<br>Ability to mitigate threats |
|---|---|---|---|---|---|---|
| Steinberg & Ritzmann, 1990 | Whereas resistance refers to the capacity of a system to maintain homeostasis, resilience refers to the capacity to implement early effective adjustment processes to alleviate strain and to return to homeostasis. | x | | x | x | |
| Twigg, 2007 | The capacity to *absorb stress or destructive forces through resistance or adaptation*; to manage or maintain certain basic functions and structures during disastrous events; and to recover or "bounce back" after an event. | x | x | | x | |

**Table B.2**
**Capacity-Based Definitions**

| Source | Capacity Definitions | Element 1: Level of community knowledge about threats | Element 2: Level of community engagement/empowerment to address risks | Element 3: Existence of social networks for response and recovery | Element 4: Existence of trust in government or public health |
|---|---|---|---|---|---|
| Berke & Campanella, 2006 | Achieving resiliency in a disaster context means the ability to survive future natural disasters with minimum loss of life and property, as well as the ability to create a greater sense of place among residents; a stronger, more diverse economy; and a more economically integrated and diverse population. *Resiliency also applies to the process of recovery planning in which all affected stakeholders—rather than just a powerful few—have a voice in how their community is to be rebuilt.* | | x | | |
| Pfefferbaum et al., 2007 | Community resilience is grounded in the *ability of community members to take meaningful, deliberate, collective action to remedy the effect of a problem,* including the ability to interpret the environment, intervene, and move on. Community resilience–building is a population-based prevention approach with implications for individuals and groups within the community. | x | x | | |
| Schoch-Spana, 2008 | Where local civic leaders, citizens and families are educated *regarding threats and are empowered to mitigate their own risk,* where they are practiced in responding to events, where they *have social networks to fall back upon,* and where they have *familiarity with local public health and medical systems,* there will be community resilience that will significantly attenuate the requirement for additional assistance. | x | x | x | |
| Schoch-Spana, 2008 | Community resilience is the ability of a community to rebound from a disaster with a new focus on recovery and mitigation and a renewed *sense of trust in government* and other community leadership. | | | | x |

# Community Prioritization Tool—Example

This tool can be used by community planning groups as they review the roadmap. It can be organized by lever and element. An example with sample response options is provided below. Please note that response options should be further specified based on community needs and context.

**Lever = Wellness**
***Element = Promote public understanding of health and wellness***

| | |
|---|---|
| What are we doing to address this element? | |
| Are there gaps in what we are doing? (y/n) | ☐ Yes <br> ☐ No |
| If yes, what kind of gaps? | ☐ We aren't reaching the populations we need to. <br> ☐ We need to do more on a routine basis. <br> ☐ We have not tested what we are doing. |
| If yes, what activities could we be doing or enhancing (see lever chapter for ideas)? | Activity 1 = _____ <br> Activity 2 = _____ |
| If yes, is it feasible to do this activity? (y/n) | ☐ Yes <br> ☐ No |
| What would make it easier? (partnerships, building on something we are already doing) | ☐ We need other partnerships. <br> ☐ We can build on a program we already have. <br> ☐ We can only do this with more funding. |
| How important is this element to our overall plans? | 1 = very important. <br> 2 = somewhat important. <br> 3 = not as critical right now. <br><br> *Note: Once you are done with this exercise, consider plans for the #1 elements first.* |

# Examples of Sample Community Resilience Measures

This appendix summarizes a sample of measures that could be used to assess progress on each of the community resilience–building levers. This includes the possible metric and potential data source. See Chapter Eleven for introductory information.

**Wellness: Promote pre- and post-incident population health, including behavioral health.**

| Subject | Measure | Data Source |
| --- | --- | --- |
| Disability status | % of population with a disability (and subset % that is homebound) | Census data |
| Poverty | % of population below the poverty line | Census data |
| Health status | % of population with good self-reported physical and mental health | BRFSS (Behavioral Risk Factor Surveillance System) |

**Access: Ensure access to high-quality health, behavioral health, and social services.**

| Subject | Measure | Data Source |
| --- | --- | --- |
| Health insurance | % of the population that has health insurance | BRFSS |

**Education: Ensure ongoing information to the public about preparedness, risks, and resources before, during, and after a disaster.**

| Subject | Measure | Data Source |
| --- | --- | --- |
| Communication vulnerability | % of households that are non-English-speaking | Census data |
| Health literacy | % of population with high school education or above | Census data |
| Health literacy | % of population with intermediate or proficient health literacy | Requires new data collection |

**Engagement: Promote participatory decisionmaking in planning, response, and recovery activities.**

| Subject | Measure | Data Source |
| --- | --- | --- |
| Identification of at-risk individuals through governmental and nongovernmental engagement | The local health department/health district has worked with organizations serving at-risk individuals to determine the number and location of at-risk individuals in the jurisdiction who are likely to be isolated during a disaster. (yes/no) | Requires new data collection |
| Identification of at-risk population "hot spots" | The local health department/health district has worked with organizations serving at-risk individuals to determine the number and location of at-risk individuals in the jurisdiction who are likely to be isolated during a disaster. (yes/no) | Requires new data collection |

| | | |
|---|---|---|
| Identification of organizations that can serve "hot spots" | The health department/health district has identified an organization that can serve as a broker of communications, services (e.g., transportation), and other resources in a disaster for each unique "hot spot" (yes/no) | Requires new data collection |
| Connectedness of general population | % of population that is affiliated with a community-based organization (e.g., church, volunteer organization) that they can rely on in an incident | Requires new data collection |
| Connectedness of general population | % of population that reports getting social support that they need. "How often do you get the social and emotional support you need?" | BRFSS |
| Voting behavior | % of eligible voters that voted in the last presidential election | Census data |

## Self-Sufficiency: Enable and support individuals and communities to assume responsibility for their preparedness.

| Subject | Measure | Data Source |
|---|---|---|
| Education with at-risk populations | % of at-risk population segments (represented by individuals or identified organizations that serve them) with which the health department has tested a risk communication message in the past year. | Requires new data collection |
| Ability to act upon official messages/ vulnerability | % of population that is willing/able to evacuate under a mandatory evacuation order | BRFSS |
| Citizen preparedness | % of population that has an emergency plan. % of population that has stockpiled supplies for use in a disaster | FEMA Citizen Corps survey and various local surveys |

## Partnership: Develop strong partnerships within and between government and nongovernmental organizations.

| Subject | Measure | Data Source |
|---|---|---|
| Local Emergency Planning Committee (LEPC) composition | Nongovernmental organizations are available to serve the HHS-defined at-risk population segments represented within the local emergency planning committee. (yes/no) | Requires new data collection |
| Role of NGOs in community response and recovery plans | % of nongovernmental local emergency planning committee members representing HHS-defined at-risk population segments with at least one acknowledged, defined, and measurable role in community disaster response and/or recovery plans | Requires new data collection |

## Quality and Efficiency: Collect, analyze, and utilize data to monitor and evaluate progress on building community resilience; leverage existing community resources for maximum effectiveness.

| Subject | Measure | Data Source |
|---|---|---|
| Time to new normalcy | Time for the community to return to pre-incident levels of functioning in the areas of human recovery, infrastructure recovery, and economic recovery | Requires new data collection |
| Integrating lessons learned | % of after-action report items addressed in subsequent planning activities | Requires new data collection |

# Bibliography

Abramson, D., Stehling-Ariza, T., Garfield, R., & Redlener, I. (2008). Prevalence and predictors of mental health distress post-Katrina: Findings from the Gulf Coast Child and Family Health Study. *Disaster Medicine and Public Health Preparedness, 2*(2), 77–86.

Aghabakhshi, H., & Gregor, C. (2007). Learning the lessons of Bam: The role of social capital. *International Social Work, 50*(3), 347–356.

Ahern, J., & Galea, S. (2006). Social context and depression after a disaster: The role of income inequality. *Journal of Epidemiology and Community Health, 60,* 766–770.

Aldrich, N., & Benson, W. F. (2008). Disaster preparedness and the chronic disease needs of vulnerable older adults. *Preventing Chronic Disease, 5*(1), A27.

Allenby, B., & Fink, J. (2005). Toward inherently secure and resilient societies. *Science, 309*(5737), 1034–1036.

Andrulis, D. P., Siddiqui, N. J., & Gantner, J. L. (2007). Preparing racially and ethnically diverse communities for public health emergencies. *Health Affairs, 26*(5), 1269–1279.

AufderHeide, E. (2004). Common misconceptions about disasters: Panic, the "disaster syndrome," and looting. In M. O'Leary, ed, *The First 72 Hours: A Community Approach to Disaster Preparedness.* Lincoln, NE: iUniverse Publishing.

Baezconde-Garbanati, L., Unger, J., Portugal, C., Delgado, J. L., Falcon, A., & Gaitan, M. (2006). Maximizing participation of Hispanic community-based/non-governmental organizations (NGOs) in emergency preparedness. *International Quarterly of Community Health Education, 24*(4), 289–317.

Baker, D., & Refsgaard, K. (2007). Institutional development and scale matching in disaster response management. *Ecological Economics, 63,* 331–343.

Beaudoin, C. E. (2007). News, social capital and health in the context of Katrina. *Journal of Healthcare for the Poor and Underserved, 18,* 418–430.

Benight, C. C., & Harper, M. L. (2002). Coping self-efficacy perceptions as a mediator between acute stress response and long-term distress following natural disasters. *Journal of Traumatic Stress, 15*(3), 177–186.

Benight, C. C., Ironson, G., Klebe, K., Carver, C. S., Wynings, C., Baum, A., et al. (1999). Conservation of resources and coping self-efficacy predicting distress following a natural disaster: A causal model analysis where the environment meets the mind. *Anxiety, Stress, and Coping, 12,* 107–126.

Berke, P. R., & Campanella, T. J. (2006). Planning for postdisaster resiliency. *Annals of the American Academy of Political and Social Science, 604*(1), 192–207.

Birmes, P., Raynaud, J.-P., Daubisse, L., Brunet, A., Arbus, C., Klein, R. M., et al. (2009). Children's enduring PTSD symptoms are related to their family's adaptability and cohesion. *Community Mental Health Journal, 45,* 290–299.

Blanchard, J. C., Haywood, Y., Stein, B. D., Tanielian, T. L., Stoto, M., & Lurie, N. (2005). In their own words: Lessons learned from those exposed to anthrax. *American Journal of Public Health, 95*(3), 489–495.

Bonanno, G. A. (2004). Loss, trauma, and human resilience: Have we underestimated the human capacity to thrive after extremely aversive events? *American Psychologist, 59*(1), 20–28.

Braun, B. I., Wineman, N. V., Finn, N. L., Barbera, J. A., Schmaltz, S. P., & Loeb, J. M. (2006). Integrating hospitals into community emergency preparedness planning. *Annals of Internal Medicine, 144*(11), 799–811.

Brodie, M., Weltzien, E., Altman, D., Blendon, R. J., & Benson, J. M. (2006). Experiences of Hurricane Katrina evacuees in Houston shelters: Implications for future planning. *American Journal of Public Health, 96*(8), 1402–1408.

Brownson, R., Fielding, J., & Maylahn, C. (2009). Evidence-based public health: A fundamental concept for public health practice. *Annual Review of Public Health, 30*, 175–201.

Bruneau, M., Chang, S. E., Eguchi, R. T., Lee, G. C., O'Rourke, T. D., Reinhorn, A. M., et al. (2003). A framework to quantitatively assess and enhance the seismic resilience of communities. *Earthquake Spectra, 19*(4), 733–752.

Buckland, J., & Rahman, M. (1999). Community-based disaster management during the 1997 Red River Flood in Canada. *Disasters, 23*(2), 174–191.

Business Executives for National Security. (2009). Building a resilient America: A proposal to strengthen public-private collaboration. As of January 23, 2010:
www.bens.org

CARRI—*See* Community and Regional Resilience Institute.

Carter-Pokras, O., Zambrana, R. E., Mora, S. E., & Aaby, K. A. (2007). Emergency preparedness: Knowledge and perceptions of Latin American immigrants. *Journal of Healthcare for the Poor and Underserved, 18*(2), 465–481.

Centers for Disease Control and Prevention & Office of Minority Health and Health Disparities (OMHD). (2009). About minority health [electronic version]. As of April 28, 2009:
http://www.cdc.gov/omhd/AMH/AMH.htm

Chandra, A., & Acosta, J. (2009). *The Role of Nongovernmental Organizations in Long-Term Human Recovery After Disaster: Reflections from Louisiana Four Years After Hurricane Katrina.* Santa Monica, CA: RAND Corporation, OP-277-RC. As of January 20, 2011:
www.rand.org/pubs/occasional_papers/OP277.html

Chandra, A., Acosta, J., Meredith, L. S., Sanches, K., Stern, S., Uscher-Pines, L., Williams, M., & Yeung, D. (2010). *Understanding Community Resilience in the Context of National Health Security: A Literature Review.* Santa Monica, CA: RAND Corporation. As of January 20, 2011:
http://www.rand.org/pubs/working_papers/WR737.html

Chen, A. C. C., Keith, V. M., Leong, K. J., Airriess, C., Li, W., Chung, K. Y., et al. (2007). Hurricane Katrina: Prior trauma, poverty and health among Vietnamese-American survivors. *54*(4), 324–331.

Ciottone, G. R., Old, A., Nicholas, S., & Anderson, P. D. (2005). Implementation of an emergency and disaster medical response training network in the commonwealth of independent states. *Journal of Emergency Medicine, 29*(2), 221–229.

Comfort, L. K. (2005). Risk, security, and disaster management. *Annual Review of Political Science, 8*, 335–356.

Committee on Risk Perception and Communication & National Research Council. (1989). *Improving Risk Communication.* Washington, DC: National Academies Press.

Community and Regional Resilience Institute. (n.d.). Definition of community resilience: What is community resilience? As of October 23, 2009:
http://www.resilientus.org/about-us/definition-of-community-resilience.html

Cordasco, K. M., Eisenman, D. P., Glik, D. C., Golden, J. F., & Asch, S. M. (2007). "They blew the levee": Distrust of authorities among Hurricane Katrina evacuees. *Journal of Healthcare for the Poor and Underserved, 18*, 277–282.

Curtis, A., Mills, J. W., & Leitner, M. (2007). Katrina and vulnerability: The geography of stress. *Journal of Healthcare for the Poor and Underserved, 18*, 315–330.

Cutter, S. L., Barnes, L., Berry, M., Burton, C., Evans, E., Tate, E., et al. (2008). A place-based model for understanding community resilience to natural disasters. *Global Environmental Change, 18*, 598–606.

Cutter, S. L., Boruff, B. J., & Shirley, W. L. (2003). Social vulnerability to environmental hazards. *Social Science Quarterly, 84*(2), 242–261.

Cutter, S. L., Mitchell, J. T., & Scott, M. S. (2000). Revealing the vulnerability of people and places: A case study of Georgetown County, South Carolina. *Annals of the Association of American Geographers, 90*(4), 713–737.

Dawes, S. S., Cresswell, A. M., & Cahan, B. B. (2004). Learning from crisis: Lessons in human and information infrastructure from the World Trade Center response. *Social Science Computer Review, 22*(1), 52–66.

DHS—*See* U.S. Department of Homeland Security.

Dobalian, A. P., Tsao, J. C., Putzer, G. J., & Menendez, S. M. (2007). Improving rural community preparedness for the chronic health consequences of bioterrorism and other public health emergencies. *Journal of Public Health Management and Practice, 13*(5), 476–480.

Dynes, R. R. (2006). Social capital: Dealing with community emergencies. *Homeland Security Affairs, 2*(2), 1–26.

Eisenman, D. P., Glik, D., Gonzalez, L., Maranon, R., Zhou, Q., Tseng, C.-H., et al. (2009). Improving Latino disaster preparedness using social networks. *American Journal of Preventive Medicine, 37*(6), 512–517.

Elmore, D. L., & Brown, L. M. (2008). Emergency preparedness and response: Health and social policy implication for older adults. *Generations, 31*(4), 66–74.

Executive Office of The President, & National Science and Technology Council. (2005). *Grand Challenges for Disaster Reduction*. Washington, DC.

Federal Emergency Management Agency. (2004). *Are You Ready? An In-Depth Guide to Citizen Preparedness*. As of August 20, 2010:
http://www.citizencorps.gov/ready/

———. (2011). Ready: Prepare, Plan, Stay Informed. As of January 28, 2011:
http://www.ready.gov/

FEMA—*See* Federal Emergency Management Agency.

Fernandez, L. S., Byard, D., Lin, C. C., Benson, S., & Barbera, J. A. (2002). Frail elderly as disaster victims: Emergency management strategies. *Prehospital and Disaster Medicine, 17*(2), 67–74.

Fothergill, A., Maestas, E., & Darlington, J. D. (1999). Race, ethnicity and disasters in the United States: A review of the literature. *Disasters, 23*(2), 156–173.

Freedman, D. A., Bess, K. D., Tucker, H. D., Boyd, D. L., Tuchman, A. M., & Wallston, K. A. (2009). Public health literacy defined. *American Journal of Preventive Medicine, 36*(5), 446–451.

Gilbert, M. (2008). Bridging the gap: Building local resilience and competencies in remote communities. *Prehospital and Disaster Medicine, 23*(4), 297–300.

Gursky, E. A. (2004). *Hometown Hospitals: The Weakest Link? Bioterrorism Readiness in America's Rural Hospitals*. Washington, DC: National Defense University, Center for Technology and National Security Policy.

Gurwitch, R. H., Pfefferbaum, B., Montgomery, J. M., Klopm, R. W., & Reissman, D. B. (2007). *Building Community Resilience for Children and Families*. Oklahoma City, OK: National Child Traumatic Stress Network.

Haines, V. A., Hurlbert, J. S., & Beggs, J. J. (1996). Exploring the determinants of support provision: Provider characteristics, personal networks, community contexts, and support following life events. *Journal of Health and Social Behavior, 37*(3), 252–264.

Helsloot I, Ruitenberg A. (2004). Citizen response to disasters: A survey of literature and some practical implications. *Journal of Contingencies and Crisis Management. 12*(3), 98–111.

HHS—*See* U.S. Department of Health and Human Services.

Hobfoll, S. E., Watson, P., Bell, C. C., Bryant, R. A., Brymer, M. J., Friedman, M. J., et al. (2007). Five essential elements of immediate and mid-term mass trauma intervention: Empirical evidence. *Psychiatry, 7*(2), 221–242.

Hurlbert, J. S., Haines, V. A., & Beggs, J. J. (2000). Core networks and tie Activation: What kinds of routine networks allocate resources in nonroutine situations? *American Sociological Review, 65*(4), 598–618.

Jacob, B., Mawson, A., Payton, M., & Guignard J. (2008). Disaster mythology and fact: Hurricane Katrina and social attachment. *Public Health Reports. 123*(5), 555–566.

Joshi, P. T., & Lewin, S. M. (2004). Disaster, terrorism, and children: Addressing the effects of traumatic events on children and their families is critical to long-term recovery and resilience. *Psychiatric Annals, 34*(9), 710–716.

Kailes, J. I., & Enders, A. (2007). Moving beyond "special needs": A function-based framework for emergency management and planning. *Journal of Disability Policy Studies, 17*(4), 230–237.

Kapila, M., McGarry, N., Emerson, E., Fink, S., Doran, R., Rejto, K., et al. (2005). Health aspects of the tsunami disaster in Asia. *Prehospital and Disaster Medicine, 20*(6), 368–377.

Kayman, H., & Ablorh-Odjidja, A. (2006). Revisiting public health preparedness: Incorporating social justice principles into pandemic preparedness planning for influenza. *Journal of Public Health Management and Practice, 12*(4), 373–380.

Keim, M. E. (2008). Building human resilience: The role of public health preparedness and response as an adaptation to climate change. *American Journal of Preventive Medicine, 35*(5), 508–516.

Kim Y., & Kang J. (2010). Communication, neighborhood belonging, and household hurricane preparedness. *Disasters, 34*(2), 470–488.

Kopp, J. B., Ball, L. K., Cohen, A., Kenney, R. J., Lempert, K. D., Miller, P. E., et al. (2007). Kidney patient care in disasters: Emergency planning for patients and dialysis facilities. *Clinical Journal of the American Society of Nephrology, 2*, 825–838.

Ku, L., & Matani, S. (2001). Left out: Immigrants' access to healthcare and insurance. *Health Affairs, 20*(1), 247–256.

Laditka, S. B., Laditka, J. N., Cornman, C. B., Davis, C. B., & Richter, J. V. (2009). Resilience and challenges among staff of gulf coast nursing homes sheltering frail evacuees following Hurricane Katrina, 2005: Implications for planning and training. *Prehospital and Disaster Medicine, 24*(1), 54–62.

Lahad, M. (2005). Terrorism: The community perspective. *Journal of Aggression, Maltreatment and Trauma, 10*(3), 667–379.

Leggiere P. Big gaps remain in citizen preparation. *HSToday.* 8–28–10, 2009.

Lindsay, J. (2003). The determinants of disaster vulnerability: Achieving sustainable mitigation through population health. *Natural Hazards, 28*, 291–304

Lyn, K., and Martin , J. A. (1991). Enhancing citizen participation: Panel designs, perspectives and policy formation. *Journal of Policy Analysis and Management, 10*(1), 46–63.

Maese, J. (2009). Medical society's blueprint for a successful community response to emergency preparedness. *Prehospital and Disaster Medicine, 24*(1), 73–75.

Magsino, S. L. (2009). *Applications of social network analysis for building community disaster resilience.* Washington, DC: National Academy of Sciences.

Manyena, S. B. (2006). The concept of resilience revisited. *Disasters, 30*(4), 434–450.

Masten, A. S., & Obradovic, J. (2008). Disaster preparation and recovery: Lessons from research on resilience in human development. *Ecology and Society, 13*(1).

Mays, G. (2010). Understanding the organization of public health delivery systems: An empirical typology. *Milbank Quarterly, 88*, 81–111.

McGee, S., Bott, C., Gupta, V., Jones, K., & Karr A. (2009). *Public Role and Engagement in Counterterrorism Efforts: Implications of Israeli Practices for The U.S.* Arlington, VA: Homeland Security Institute. As of January 20, 2011:
http://www.homelandsecurity.org/hsireports/Public_Role_in_CT_Israeli_Practices_Task_08-22.pdf

McMillan, D. W., & Chavis, D. M. (1986). Sense of community: A definition and theory. *Journal of Community Psychology, 14*(1), 6–23.

Mechanic, D., & Tanner, J. (2007). Vulnerable people, groups, and populations: Societal view. *Health Affairs, 26*(5), 1220–1230.

Mitchell, T. L., Griffin, K., Stewart, S. H., & Loba, P. (2004). 'We will never ever forget. . . .': The Swissair Flight 111 disaster and its impact on volunteers and communities. *Journal of Health Psychology, 9*(2), 245–262.

Moore, S., Daniel, M., Linnan, L., Campbell, M., Benedict, S., & Meier, A. (2004). After Hurricane Floyd passed: Investigating the social determinants of disaster preparedness and recovery. *Family and Community Health, 27*(3), 204–217.

Morrow, B. H. (1999). Identifying and mapping community vulnerability. *Disasters, 23*(1), 1–18.

Murphy, B. L. (2007). Locating social capital in resilient community-level emergency management. *Natural Hazards, 41*, 297–315.

Nates, J. L. (2004). Combined external and internal hospital disaster: Impact and response in a Houston trauma center intensive care unit. *Critical Care Medicine, 32*(3), 686–690.

National Childhood Traumatic Stress Network. (2011). *Psychological First Aid Operations Guide.* As of January 30, 2011:
http://www.nctsnet.org/trauma-types/natural-disasters/psychological-first-aid

National Council on Disability. (2005). *Saving Lives: Including People with Disabilities in Emergency Planning.* Washington, DC: National Council on Disability.

National Research Council. (2006). *Community Disaster Resilience: A Summary of the March 20, 2006, Workshop of the Disasters Roundtable.* Washington, DC: The National Academies Press.

National Security Strategy. (2010). As of January 26, 2010:
http://www.whitehouse.gov/sites/default/files/rss_viewer/national_security_strategy.pdf

Ng, A. T. (2005). Cultural diversity in the integration of disaster mental health and public health: A case study in response to bioterrorism. *International Journal of Emergency Mental Health, 7*(1), 23–31.

Nichols, K. L. (1998). Benefits of vaccination for low-, intermediate-, and high-risk senior citizens. *Annals of Internal Medicine. 15*(6), 1769–1176.

Nielsen-Bohlman, L., Panzer, A. M., Institute of Medicine (U.S.), Committee on Health Literacy, & Kindig, D. A. (2004). *Health literacy: A prescription to end confusion.* Washington, DC: The National Academies Press.

Norris, F. H., Stevens, S. P., Pfefferbaum, B., Wyche, K. F., & Pfefferbaum, R. L. (2008). Community resilience as a metaphor, theory, set of capacities, and strategy for disaster readiness. *American Journal of Community Psychology, 41*(1–2), 127–150.

Padgett, S., Kinabrew, C., Kimbrell, J., & Nicola, R. (2005). Turning point and public health institutes: Vehicles for systems change. *Journal of Public Health Management and Practice, 11*, 116–122.

Pant, A. T., Kirsch, T. D., Subbarao, I. R., Hsieh, Y.-H., & Vu, A. (2008). Faith-based organizations and sustainable sheltering operations in Mississippi after Hurricane Katrina: Implications for informal network utilization. *Prehospital and Disaster Medicine, 23*(1), 48–54.

Paton, D., Gregg, C. E., Houghton, B. F., Lachman, R., Lachman, J., Johnston, D. M., et al. (2007). The impact of the 2004 tsunami on coastal Thai communities: Assessing adaptive capacity. *Disasters, 32*(1), 106–119.

Paton, D., Parkes, B., Daly, M., & Smith, L. (2008). Fighting the flu: Developing sustained community resilience and preparedness. *Health Promotion Practice, 9*(4 suppl), 45S–53S.

Pennel, C. L., Carpender, S. L., & Quiram, B. J. (2008). Rural health roundtables: A strategy for collaborative engagement in and between rural communities. *International Electronic Journal of Rural and Remote Health Research, Education, Practice and Policy.*

Pfefferbaum, B. J., Pfefferbaum, R. L., & Norris, F. H. (2009). Community resilience and wellness for children exposed to Hurricane Katrina. In R. P. Kilmer, V. Gil-Rivas, R. G. Tedeschi & L. G. Calhoun, eds., *Helping families and communities recover from disaster: Lessons learned from Hurricane Katrina and its aftermath* (pp. 265–288). Washington, DC: American Psychological Association.

Pfefferbaum, B. J., Reissman, D. B., Pfefferbaum, R. L., Klomp, R. W., & Gurwitch, R. H. (2005). Building resilience to mass trauma events. In L. S. Doll, S. E. Bonzo, J. A. Mercy & D. A. Sleet, eds., *Handbook on injury and violence prevention interventions.* New York: Kluwer Academic Publishers.

————. (2007). Building resilience to mass trauma events. In L. S. Doll & S. E. Bonzo, eds., *Handbook of injury and violence prevention* (pp. 347–358). New York: Springer Science+Business Media.

Pfefferbaum, R. L., Reissman, D. B., Pfefferbaum, B., Wyche, K. F., Norris, F. H., & Klamp, R. W. (2008). Factors in the development of community resilience to disasters. In M. Blumenfield & R. J. Ursano, eds., *Intervention and resilience after mass trauma* (pp. 49–68). Cambridge, England: Cambridge University Press.

Procopio, C. H., & Procopio, S. T. (2007). Do you know what it means to miss New Orleans? Internet communication, geographic community, and social capital in crisis. *Journal of Applied Communication Research, 35*(1), 67–87.

Putnam, R. D. (2000). *Bowling Alone: The Collapse and Revival of American Community.* New York: Simon and Schuster.

Quinn, S. C. (2008). Crisis and emergency risk communication in a pandemic: A model for building capacity and resilience of minority communities. *Health Promotion Practice, 9*(4_suppl), 18S–25.

Reissman, D. B., Spencer, S., Tanielian, T. L., & Stein, B. D. (2005). Integrating behavioral aspects into community preparedness and response systems. *Journal of Aggression, Maltreatment and Trauma, 10*(3–4), 707–720.

Riddell, K., & Clouse, M. (2004). Comprehensive psychosocial emergency management promotes recovery. *International Journal of Emergency Mental Health, 6*(3), 135–145.

Ringel, J. A, Chandra A., Williams, M., Ricci, K., Felton, A., et al. (2009). *Enhancing Public Health Preparedness Planning for Special Needs Populations: A Toolkit for State and Local Planning and Response* (includes interactive GIS mapping tool). Santa Monica, CA: RAND Corporation, TR-681-DHHS. As of January 29, 2011:
http://www.rand.org/pubs/technical_reports/TR681.html

Rogers, B., & Lawhorn, E. (2007). Disaster preparedness: Occupational and environmental health professionals' response to Hurricanes Katrina and Rita. *American Association of Occupational Health Nurses Journal, 55*(5), 197–207.

Salinsky, E. (2010). *Governmental Public Health: An Overview of State and Local Public Health Agencies.* Washington, DC: National Health Policy Forum.

Schellong, A. (2007). *Increasing social capital for disaster response through social networking services (SNS) in Japanese local governments.* Arlington, VA: National Science Foundation.

Schoch-Spana, M. (2008). Community resilience for catastrophic health events. *Biosecurity and Bioterrorism: Biodefense Strategy, Practice, and Science, 6*(2), 129–130.

Schultz, C. H., Jerry, L. M., & Field, M. (2002). Bioterrorism preparedness I: The emergency department and hospital. *Emergency medicine clinics of North America, 20*(2), 437–455.

Southeast Region Research Initiative (SERRI) and Community and Regional Resilience Institute. (2009). Creating resilient communities: The work of SERRI and CARRI. As of January 23, 2010: www.resilientus.org

Shiu-Thornton, S., Balabis, J., Senturia, K., Tamayo, A., & Oberle, M. (2007). Disaster preparedness for limited English proficient communities: Medical interpreters as cultural brokers and gatekeepers. *Public Health Reports, 122*(4), 466–471.

Simpson, D. D. (2002). A conceptual framework for transferring research to practice. *Journal of Substance Abuse Treatment, 22*, 171–182.

Sistrom, M. G., & Hale, P. J. (2006). Outbreak investigations: Community participation and role of community and public health nurses. *Public Health Nursing, 23*(3), 256–263.

Steinberg, A., & Ritzmann, R. F. (1990). A living systems approach to understanding the concept of stress. *Behavioral Science, 35*(2), 138–146.

Steury, S., Spencer, S., & Parkinson, G. W. (2004). The social context of recovery. *Psychiatry, 67*(2), 158–163.

Stewart, G. T., Kolluru, R., & Smith, M. (2009). Leveraging public-private partnerships to improve community resilience in times of disaster. *International Journal of Physical Distribution and Logistics Management, 39*(5), 343–364.

Subcommittee on Economic Development, Public Buildings, and Emergency Management. (2009). Hearing, Post Katrina: What It Takes to Cut the Bureaucracy. Washington, DC.

Sutherland, K., Christianson, J. B., & Leatherman, S. (2008). Impact of targeted financial incentives on personal health behavior: A review of literature. *Medical Care Research and Review 65*(6 Suppl), 36S–78S.

Twigg, J. (2007). *Characteristics of a Disaster-Resilient Community: A Guidance Note*: DFID Disaster Risk Reduction Interagency Coordination Group.

Terrorism and Disaster Center, University of Oklahoma Health Sciences Center. (2010). Community Advancing Resilience Toolkit (CART). As of November 29, 2010: http://www.oumedicine.com/Workfiles/College%20of%20Medicine/AD-Psychiatry/CART_description_021510.pdf

Ursano, R. J., Fullerton, C. S., Benedek, D. M., & Hamaoka, D. A. (2007). Hurricane Katrina: Disasters teach us and we must learn. *Academic Psychiatry 31*, 180–182, May–June.

U.S. Department of Health & Human Services. (n.d.) *HHS Pandemic Influenza Plan Supplement 11 Workforce Support: Psychosocial Considerations and Information Needs.* Washington, DC.

———. (2009). *National Health Security Strategy of the United States of America.* Washington, DC. As of January 26, 2011: http://www.phe.gov/Preparedness/planning/authority/nhss/strategy/Pages/default.aspx

———. (2010a). HHS Recovery CONOPS. As of February 9, 2011: http://www.phe.gov/Preparedness/support/conops/Pages/default.aspx

———. (2010b). *Biennial Implementation Plan for the National Health Security Strategy of the United States of America,* Washington, DC, Draft, July 29.

U.S. Department of Homeland Security. (2007). *Homeland Security Presidential Directive/HSPD-21: Public Health and Medical Preparedness.* Washington, DC.

——— (2010). Draft National Disaster Recovery Framework. February 5.

Varda, D. M., Chandra, A., Stern, S. A., & Lurie, N. (2008). Core dimensions of connectivity in public health collaboratives. *Journal of Public Health Management and Practice, 14*(5), E1–E7.

Varda, D. M., Forgette, R., Banks, D., & Contractor, N. (2009). Social network methodology in the study of disasters: Issues and insights prompted by post-Katrina research. *Population Research and Policy Review, 28*, 11–29.

Walker, K. L., & Chestnut, D. (2003). The role of ethnocultural variables in response to terrorism. *Cultural Diversity and Ethnic Minority Psychology, 9*(3), 251–262.

Walsh, F. (2007). Traumatic loss and major disasters: Strengthening family and community resilience. *Family Process, 46*(2), 207–227.

Weems, C. F., Wattsa, S. E., Marseeb, M. A., Taylora, L. K., Costaa, N. M., Cannona, M. F., et al. (2007). The psychosocial impact of Hurricane Katrina: Contextual differences in psychological symptoms, social support, and discrimination. *Behaviour Research and Therapy, 45*, 2295–2306.

Weycker, D., Edelsberg, M., Halloran, E., Longini, I. M., Nizam, A., Ciuryla, V., & Oster, G. (2005). Population-wide benefits of routine vaccination of children against influenza. *Vaccine*, 23, 1284–1293.

Williams, J. C. (2008). State of emergency preparedness of Kentucky's rural public health workforce: Assessing its ability to identify community health problems. *Public Health Reports, 123*, 178–188.

Wingate, M. S., Perry, E. C., Campbell, P. H., David, P., & Weist, E. M. (2007). Identifying and protecting vulnerable populations in public health emergencies: Addressing gaps in education and training. *Public Health Reports, 122*(3), 422–426.

Wise, G. I. (2007). Preparing for disaster: A way of developing community relationships. *Disaster Management and Response, 5*(1), 14–17.

Yong-Chan, K., & Jinae, K. (2010). Communication, neighbourhood belonging and household hurricane preparedness. *Disasters, 34*(2), 289–591.

Zarcadoolas, C., Krishnaswami, A., Boyer, J., & Rothenberg, A. (2007). GIS maps to communicate emergency preparedness: How useable are they for inner city residents? *Journal of Homeland Security and Emergency Management, 4*(3), 1–14.